THANK YOU
FOR SUPPORTING
MENTAL HEALTH.

MW01015637

THE UNBROKEN

A FIREFIGHTER'S MEMOIR

STEVE SERBIC

 FriesenPress

Suite 300 - 990 Fort St
Victoria, BC, V8V 3K2
Canada

www.friesenpress.com

ISBN
978-1-5255-9887-6 (Hardcover)
978-1-5255-9886-9 (Paperback)
978-1-5255-9888-3 (eBook)

1. BIOGRAPHY & AUTOBIOGRAPHY, PERSONAL MEMOIRS

Distributed to the trade by The Ingram Book Company

ABOUT THE BOOK

When a series of traumatic calls on the job as a firefighter leaves Steve shaken and unable to recover, he, reluctantly at first, seeks out clinical counselling. His one rule, "I won't talk about my childhood," closes the door on several therapists, until he meets one who is willing to respect his wishes—providing he explores his childhood on his own. When Steve begins to reflect on his past, he also begins to write it all down. The good, and the terrible.

Those written words are here.

Growing up in a fractured family rocked by addiction and trauma, Steve had to learn how to understand life, and death, on his own. As a self-described "street rat" on Boundary Road in East Vancouver, Steve caused trouble when it wasn't already following him around. Struggling in school, at home, and in countless fights, he navigated his way through adolescence with the help of his father, and pursued his dream of becoming a firefighter. While realizing that dream, he is forced to confront the demons of his past and the reality of post-traumatic stress injury. Through clinical counselling he is able to release his past and find the power of self-acceptance and vulnerability. The Unbroken is the memoir of one firefighter, his family, trauma, and resilience. Most importantly it is a story that teaches all of us, no matter our situation, that life is school, and the subject is ourself, our life habits, thoughts, and our reactions to them. And that sometimes it is okay to not be okay.

For Helen, Nikolas and Danika.
And for Ken Gill.

PREFACE

I said there was one thing I would never do in my career as a firefighter. I would never be a chief. Yet there I was in 2015, newly hired as an assistant chief far from home in a department that I thought I could just fit into, because I was from a big city department.

I was so wrong. I was considered an outsider.

In the first few days with Esquimalt Fire, I knew it was going to be challenging. My family remained home in the North Shore area of Vancouver and I commuted for the first year — going back and forth on ferries or floatplanes. I'd work four days on and go home on my four days off. My official title was Assistant Chief of Operations but I quickly realized that the firefighters didn't trust me. I was mostly ignored, and they didn't speak to me for months. Even on calls, they rarely talked with me. A couple of senior firefighters gave me a hard time — always confrontational. Perhaps they were angry that two internal candidates who had applied did not get the job, and now an outsider was supervising on the management level. I didn't know the exact reasons, but I certainly felt unwelcome the first few months on the job.

You know, when I decided I wanted to be a chief, I really wanted to be a different kind of chief, one that could make a difference by improving firefighter mental health. Just a few months before, my former department, Surrey Fire, had two firefighter suicides in seven weeks. I was sensitive to this fact — it left me rattled. Surely as a chief, I could help to make change; help to break the stigma of the macho firefighter, never appearing weak, always saving others while hiding their own struggles with what they witnessed.

As a firefighter, I had worked for many captains and chiefs who were open to listening. At Esquimalt Fire, I wanted to be the guy with an open-door policy where anyone could come and talk to me if they weren't feeling strong, or something was wrong. I would listen. I would help them seek counselling. From my own experience, I learned that a mental health professional was critical to processing job stress and depression; how healing it was to be in a safe place to talk.

At Esquimalt Fire, I soon realized my idea for an open-door policy was not a shoe-in. The firefighters were skeptical — management was viewed as other than 'brother' and the fire chief had not endorsed any type of mental health program. I was seriously questioning my decision to stay with the department.

Then a man named Ken reached out to me. He was a retired captain who had returned to Oak Bay Fire as a volunteer chaplain in 2015. A strong man of faith, Ken was committed to his role in supporting the health and well-being of firefighters and their families. He heard I was struggling and suggested we meet for coffee. I will never forget the big smile on his face or his first words asking how I was doing although he already knew the answer. Instinctively I trusted him, and we talked for a couple of hours. Ken was kind and sensitive to what I was telling him.

He had a calming effect on me, and I felt he sincerely cared. Over the course of more meetings, Ken made many helpful suggestions on how to build trust with my firefighters, which in turn improved my self-confidence in the role of assistant chief. I gradually became more comfortable in the job, thanks to Ken. I don't think I would have stuck it out if he hadn't come into my life.

One day a call came in from a firefighter in a regional department. I had spoken with him several times, and knew he was struggling. I had talked with him before about his mental health and he wanted to thank me for that. He was clearly upset and I immediately asked, "Are you ok?"

He paused and didn't answer.

"Are you thinking of harming yourself?"

He answered, "I am going to commit suicide."

I wasn't sure what to do, besides calling 911. I spoke with him for about half an hour until his wife came home, and then I got Ken on the phone. He drove to the firefighter's home and spent the day with him, advising his wife when to call 911. At 3:30 in the morning, this firefighter attempted to take his life. His wife made the call and he was rushed to hospital.

I discussed this incident with Ken and told him how upsetting it was. I never again wanted to receive a call from a firefighter threatening suicide and not know how to handle it. He agreed. I said I wanted to take a stand by putting myself out there — telling firefighters: *it is okay to not be okay*. I had lived the experience of depression and suicidal thoughts in the past and recovered with the guidance of a very good clinical counsellor. I wanted to speak out as a mental health advocate, and Ken offered to assist as a volunteer chaplain for Esquimalt in addition to Oak Bay. Over the next year, Ken and I developed connections with several clinical counsellors, trauma doctors, and wellness professionals. I started telling my personal story to groups of fire-fighter crews to challenge the stigma (sign of weakness) attached to mental health. I also made dozens of presentations to high school students—I had witnessed some very tragic outcomes in incidents involving teenagers.

The local branch of BC Mental Health had started a suicide-safe talk program and Ken hosted one at the Oak Bay fire hall. Chiefs and firefight-ers attended from over a dozen fire departments. Pandora's box had opened. Calls started to come in from people wanting to ask questions or tell us their stories. It was obvious there were many firefighters quietly struggling. We were not the only ones who had gone through periods of depression and suicidal thoughts. Ken and I agreed to keep all these calls confidential and not share them between us.

I was taking about a dozen calls per month, and gradually gaining a repu-tation for being trustworthy. Ken, as a well-known chaplain, answered an average of thirty to fifty calls and would still meet with another forty-eight firefighters on a regular basis between Oak Bay and

Esquimalt. It was extremely demanding. Although he didn't say anything to me, to carry the burden of so many stories of trauma in confidence had to be overwhelming at times.

By November of 2017, my firefighters seemed happier and my job was going well. I was enjoying my role in charge of operations even though big calls were few-and-far between. Toward the end of the month, things took a turn for the worse — we got a call for a hanging. I didn't normally go to medical calls, but this was the second hanging in a short period of time. The previous hanging was a friend of the crew captain, so this time I made sure I was part of the call to better support the crew. It was a 16-year-old boy bullied at school. The family was in the house when the crew arrived. It was a traumatizing scene.

When the crew got back to the hall, I gave them time to settle down, then sat them around the table and gave out phone numbers to call for confidential counselling services. I explained how they might feel over the next few days and encouraged them to talk with their spouses but to leave out details of the scene; there is often an adverse effect on the spouse. I suggested the crew go down to the marina area, grab a coffee, and take a walk. Though they were on duty, I did not expect them to do daily drills or inspections. They were grateful.

Ken came by on November 23 and spent a couple of hours with the crew. Afterward, we talked for over an hour in my office. He asked if I was okay and said I looked tired. Some of the guys had told him I was snapping at them. I walked around my desk and gave Ken a big bear hug. I told him there had been a bit of a blow-up between a couple of firefighters and me, but it was all good now and I was fine.

I was lying. I was not fine; I wasn't sleeping, but I didn't want to tell Ken. The hanging call had triggered memories of the many gruesome hangings I had attended as a Surrey firefighter. Ken looked tired as well and I knew his plate was full. I did not want to add my problem. As he was leaving, he turned and asked, "Are you sure you're okay?" I frowned and said, "Ken, you're the department chaplain, would I lie to you?" He burst out laughing and said, "Okay, but you know I'm always available." That was the last time I saw my friend, Ken.

On December 25, Oak Bay Fire was called to one of the grizzliest murder scenes in the region's history. A father with shared custody of his two little girls, aged four and six, had stabbed both of them multiple times until they were dead. First responders found the father alive lying in the bathtub with stab wounds to his neck and chest. When the firefighters returned to the hall, Ken communicated with them. Since December 4, on his doctor's advice, Ken was taking time off to care for his own mental health. Not being there in person to support the firefighters really bothered him; but over the phone, he listened and relived the call with each responding fire fighter. It was Christmas Day.

I texted Ken a belated holiday message wishing him and his family all the best. He returned the same greetings to me and my family. On January 1, I texted wishing him a Happy New Year. This time he responded that he was struggling and was taking some time off. He answered a second message I sent on January 7: "Thanks for everything Steve, but I won't be communicating for the next few weeks." I knew he was in trouble and said, "There is so much love for you Ken … fight this and remember how many people are here to help you."

In the third week of January, Ken was having very dark thoughts and spent a few days in hospital. On February 15 he attempted suicide. Just in time, his wife managed to call 911 and save his life. Ken was hospitalized in the psychiatric ward at Victoria's Royal Jubilee. After some time, he was put on watch in another ward. Forty-two days later, a doctor, without consulting Ken's wife, allowed him a two-hour pass from the hospital. Ken walked from the hospital to downtown Victoria, climbed the stairs to the roof of the tallest parkade in the city, and jumped. He died on March 29, 2018.

Ken and I had spent hours discussing our personal mental health concerns, including intermittent thoughts of suicide, but when the chips were down in late December, we failed to tell each other what was really going on. We didn't open up. Instead, we kept up the stoic façade of being in control … that everything was fine and we were okay … when we were not.

I lost my teacher, mentor and friend, but his voice stays with me. I will continue Ken's work: the effort necessary for changing Fire culture from one that disdains vulnerability to one that embraces and prioritizes strong mental health for its members; a culture where firefighters and family members are encouraged to access confidential counselling and speak freely about their worries in a safe place.

In the pages that follow, I tell my story of growing up in a truly dysfunctional family with parents whose alcohol addiction interfered with any childhood sense of stability and security.

My mother's unwillingness to face her demons with anything other than alcohol, and my father's refusal to go against her, tore the family apart. Our way of living failed my half-brother who eventually took his own life; and yet ironically primed me for the mental toughness a career firefighter needs to survive.

CHAPTER ONE

Nothing Good Happens After Midnight

2001 April 20th 23:37 Firehouse #10, Surrey, BC

"Engine 10, Engine 10 — respond to 7351 Hall Road
for a man stuck in a tree, I repeat Engine 10 respond to
7351 Hall Road for a man stuck in a tree, over."

Having just crawled into bed and fallen asleep, we get the call — and it really sucks getting out of bed again. For firefighters, nothing good comes after midnight. I must be getting old, not being able to handle the switch from sleeping to screaming down the road in thirty seconds for some loser stuck up a tree. Flipping off the sheets, I ran down the stairs in my underwear, throwing on my bunker gear just outside the truck bay door. I trooped into the bay to see everyone on the truck already. As soon as they saw me, the engine started to move and I jumped into the back of the truck, the mother-in-law, as we called it. Ralph drove, with Wally in the captain's seat and Roger and me in the back.

Our call on Hall Road was just around the corner so it took less than a minute to arrive. This call was pretty simple—a guy forty-feet up a gigantic maple tree, apparently to get a cat — but this wasn't the nicest area of Surrey, and we had to keep our heads up as you never know what could happen. He also had an audience of twenty drunks screaming *Jump!* and appeared to be enjoying the attention.

"Hey, buddy, what the hell are you doing up there?" I yelled to him.

"I'm stuck, and I can't climb down."

"Sure you can, just come down the same way you went up."

"I can't." He was terrified in his reply.

All right, I thought, *the sooner I go up and help him down the quicker we get back to the firehouse, and back to bed.* It was an easy tree to climb and I could get to him in just a couple of minutes, so I grabbed some rope and headed up. As I climbed someone yelled, "Don't drop the cat!" I looked up and sure enough, the guy was holding a *fucking cat*.

I kept summiting the tree, ignoring the laughing and yelling crowd, but when I arrived at his branch, the guy, Dave, drunk, in his mid-30s, holding a fucking cat, had a huge smile on.

"Hey dude, what's with the cat?" I asked. It was stuck, he explained, and a girl wanted someone to go get it so he volunteered.

A tad pissed now, I scolded, "Cats climb up and down trees all the time, and if you would just let it go, I'm sure it will make its way back down."

"It didn't come down when they called it, so I knew it was stuck," he said.

"Okay buddy," I said, "put the cat on the branch and let's go." The cat's owner was yelling at him from below, "Don't leave my cat up there!"

This area was home to a good portion of the city's crack users. Working girls usually stood on every other corner. Tonight, however, they were all at the base of this tree watching the unfolding circus. As Dave whimpered to me, the stoned and drunken crowd below started yelling again: *Jump!*

I screamed at the crowd, "Shut up!" Then I turned to the guy in the tree and screamed right in his face, "Drop the *fucking* cat!" And he did — just let it go, mid-air. The cat fell all the way to the ground without hitting a single branch, landing on its feet and bolting off into the bushes.

"You son of a bitch!" the girl screamed. As an animal lover, it wasn't how I wanted it to go down. I was glad it survived the manhandling it had received and by this point, I was pissed at the guy and just wanted to get the hell out of there. We both climbed down only to find the cat owner waiting for me.

"You're a piece of work! What's your badge number? I'm calling the fire chief!" She went on and on … *blah, blah, blah…* and after a few minutes I ignored her, gathered up my stuff, and got back into the truck.

We arrived back at the Fire hall at 12:45 am — more than enough time to get in a couple of hours sleep before the next call. If we were lucky, the few hours might even turn into a decent night's sleep.

The greatest men and women make up the Surrey Fire Service. We usually had all kinds of fun on-shift, no matter the time of day, but at this point the department was in some serious turmoil, and night shifts were brutal. We had a new fire chief, and he was doing things never done before in any department. This chief insisted we go out after midnight in our big red trucks and drive around for a couple of hours looking for trouble, like security guards patrolling the city in the wee hours of the morning, looking for bad guys and peeking into the windows of schools.

We also had two new rescue trucks with high-capacity pumps. They were short-wheel- based fire trucks with 300 gallons of water, jaws, heavy rescue equipment, and remote-control nozzles. That's right, *remote control*, so you only need two guys to run a fire truck. You arrive, pull hose and enter the building; supposedly a cost saving measure for the department. The outcome was a bad working environment with firefighters and management not talking for over twelve months. If a chief walked by, you were to look at the ground and not acknowledge him. If he gave you an order, you were to obey, but without speaking back. So, when I say I love this job, I do — I just hated it right then. Luckily, my fire hall was one of the lucky ones getting, on average, about six calls after midnight. The slower halls would be out there wasting two hours, and I am telling you, it is a *long* two hours.

Now I'm back in bed and trying to get some sleep and the phone rings. My watch said 1:13 am. As before, for firefighters, nothing good ever happens after midnight. A phone ringing is one of the worst, and I always think the same thing: *Please don't be for me, please don't be for me.*

I heard the captain coming up the stairs — with three guys sleeping upstairs, including me, we're looking at a one-in-three chance. I pulled the covers over my head; the footsteps stopped, so I pulled them down again, and there's Wally standing over my bed.

"Steve, that was dispatch, and Engine 4 is at your home. You better call your wife." My wife Helen, a nurse, was on maternity leave and at home with our four-week-old baby daughter and four-year-old son.

"What for?" I barked.

"Infant not breathing," he said.

"What!" I yelled and leapt for the phone.

"Helen, what the hell is going on?"

My wife, crying on the other end of the phone said, "Danika stopped breathing."

"What do you mean? Why aren't you at the hospital?" I replied.

"She's okay now — but she stopped breathing — completely."

"Is the ambulance still there?" I asked calmly. I could tell Helen was a mess.

"No, everyone left. The crew from Engine 4 and the paramedics got into an argument, but she's fine now."

"I'm coming home."

It was a furious drive home. I couldn't understand what had happened: why did Danika stop breathing? And why the hell would the paramedics not take her to the hospital?

When I walked in the house, my daughter stopped breathing again right in front of me then started again after about 15 seconds. I quickly took my son, Nikolas, over to the neighbour's home, and we took off for the hospital, my wife sitting with my daughter in the back seat. Danika kept choking, then passing out, and then would just return to normal. As I drove, I couldn't get over the fact that the paramedics didn't take her to the hospital. Maybe they didn't believe Helen. Maybe they knew something I didn't. Still — what the hell?!

I dropped Helen off at the emergency entrance and parked the car. It took me only a couple of minutes before I was back in Emergency. I asked the triage nurse if she knew where my wife and baby were. She started into me: "Are you the father? What are you *thinking* driving your baby to the hospital? When a baby stops breathing, you need to call an ambulance, I don't care if you're a firefighter, *blah, blah, blah* ...." She just went on and on, and I barely let her finish before shouting, "We *did* call an ambulance — they came and left!"

That shut her up.

"Now where are my wife and daughter?" I demanded and she pointed to the back room without speaking.

We waited for an hour and, of course, Danika was fine the entire time we were there. A doctor finally came to us and said he could find nothing wrong.

After three hours with no choking or stopped breathing episodes, we were referred to our family doctor, and discharged. Helen stayed up all night keeping watch on Danika. Knowing that, I dozed off and surprisingly slept a few hours before going to the family doctor when she opened at 9:00 am. Our doctor could not find anything wrong but referred us to see a neonatologist at the same hospital as the night before. Sure enough, that guy found nothing wrong with Danika either. Between the paramedics and the three doctors we just saw, I was convinced they all thought we were overreacting. We got home at noon and Helen kept saying, *something is wrong*, that Danika is not sucking right or swallowing normally. I called the nursing station at our local Children's Hospital and as soon I described Danika's intermittent choking and non-breathing episodes, they told us to come right in. Off we went for another hospital visit.

Dr. Korn, a pediatric respiratory specialist, saw us immediately. The nurse assured us he was one of the best in the country and *was* examining Danika thoroughly. He looked at Helen and said, "She isn't presenting anything — but you're a nurse and you are very upset. I'm going to go with your instincts and admit your daughter overnight for observation."

Helen started crying. Not only had she not slept for twenty hours, but someone had finally listened.

Helen was overwhelmed and couldn't sleep a wink that night either. Danika was hooked up to a monitor, and the alarms would go off every five minutes. The nurse came in each time to say, "Don't worry about it," and then re-set the alarms.

After a long night, the lab tech came in to say they were discharging us right after a Respiratory Syncytial Virus (RSV) test was done. She said it is a very rare virus. Danika likely didn't have it, but the emergency doctor wanted to rule out the possibility. The doctor came by and said everything would be fine and, as soon as they ruled out RSV, we could go home for some much-needed rest. Helen seemed a little more settled now. Maybe, I wondered, it was a one-off thing. Maybe it would just never happen again.

The doctor came in and said he was sorry, but our daughter had RSV. Immediately, we plied him with questions. We learned it was a virus that a *child* could get over, but for infants it is *fatal*. We asked if she was going to die. He said it was hard to tell, with our daughter barely four-weeks old. They had one other infant with the virus at the time. She was on a respirator, very ill.

Helen just looked out the window. I felt like someone had kicked me in the balls. The doctor told us to prepare for a lengthy stay.

I wanted to kill those paramedic bastards who had first attended. Most fire departments and ambulance paramedics *do not* get along, but my department had never had a problem with them. Paramedics often feel that firefighters are taking away part of their job by responding to calls —but most of the ambulance crews I worked with were awesome. The paramedic who came to my home was one of the most experienced in the city, but he was decidedly full of himself. I was so pissed I wanted to hammer him — to this day, I can't understand why he would take a chance with a newborn baby.

After several days in isolation —a tiny room, no outside visitors, everyone in and out wearing masks— we decided that I should go home and return to work my four-day set and come back between shifts and be with our son. The doctor told us this could go on for weeks, maybe longer.

It was good to see Nikolas, who'd been hanging out with our good friends next door and their three girls. The next morning, I dropped our son Nik back with the neighbour, also our daycare. I was looking forward to being back on shift with my buds Wally, Ralph and Roger. I usually arrive half an hour early and tell the guy I am replacing that he can split. It was 7:15 and I was at work 45 minutes before my shift started, so I told the guy in my spot he could take off, and I was ready to take the shift. I had been seated at the galley table for five minutes when we got a call for *infant in distress*. I hopped on the rig with Roger, also early to his shift.

We arrived at a home about two miles away from the fire hall to see an older man waiting for us in the street. As we piled out, the man ran frantically into the house. Not a good sign. We followed close behind, up the stairs and into the house. I got into the bedroom first with Roger right on my ass, and on the bed was a two-or-three-month-old little baby not breathing, with no pulse, in full arrest.

I took him off the bed and placed him on the floor. As we start doing CPR and ventilations, I could hear the grandmother crying, saying that she 'only left him for a minute.' *If she says a minute*, I'm thinking, it's probably five minutes, maybe ten. She kept shrieking, "Is he okay?" as Roger and I worked on the little guy with no response. There were no signs as to how long he'd been in arrest, aside from his blue skin and lips. It could have been five minutes, and if so, then we had a chance — a slim chance. Five minutes went by, then ten minutes with no paramedics. Roger yelled to the captain to update the ambulance, trying to get them to step it up.

Fifteen minutes passed. Roger and I were dripping sweat on this little guy, just working away. If we could simulate blood flow with CPR, and then the drugs and AED from the paramedics, we still had a chance. Just as I was about to yell, "Where the hell is the ambulance?" they walked through the door. To my surprise, the same paramedic who attended my baby daughter came into the bedroom as we are doing CPR. The guy who decided not to take my baby girl, my Danika to the hospital, had just waltzed into the room. It was hard for me to remain calm and professional when he kneeled beside us and said, "Nice try guys, but the kid is a goner."

He was the senior paramedic, but I felt like exploding when he said those words.

"We are going to do the full protocol," he continued, "because we have a new paramedic — but you guys can stop CPR."

I stood up, looked him right in the eye, and walked out, kicking the door open. I heard one of the other paramedics muttering, "What's his problem?"

It wasn't the paramedics' fault my daughter contracted RSV, but she could have choked to death after they left her that night. I was furious at the guy for putting my daughter and wife through it all. Plus, Roger and I worked our butts off to revive that little boy, and Dickhead walks in like some fucking cowboy only to say, "He's a goner." What a jerk.

Back in the rig, I was visibly shaking. When the captain came back and opened the door, he could see that I was crying. He asked me if I was okay,

I said, "Yeah." Roger got in the rig and asked if I was okay, and I didn't say a word. My eyes said *get lost*. We drove all the way back from the call in silence.

Back at the hall, the crew talked about the call. Apparently, Mom and Dad hadn't had a night out in some time, so Grandma and Grandad were babysitting. The baby could not roll yet, or so the old woman thought; she left him sleeping in the middle of the queen-sized bed. Finding his way over to the wall, the little guy somehow got his head stuck between the mattress and the wall, suffocating to death. Roger told the rest of my crew that Dickhead was the paramedic who had showed up at my home, responding to my daughter.

That shift took forever. We only had five calls. I phoned my wife at the hospital ten times to see if my little girl was alright. When my shift ended, I couldn't get out of the fire house fast enough to get back to the hospital. I just had a feeling she was not going to make it. That's one of the weird things about working in emergency response: you relate all the bad things you see back to your own life and the ones you love. My daughter was sleeping peacefully, or as well as could be expected with all the wires and monitors connected to her. I left the hospital at 10:30 that night with a bad feeling about her recovery.

I made it home quite late and grabbed Nikolas from the neighbour's house just before midnight and shuffled him into bed. The department shifts were two ten-hour day shifts, followed by two fourteen-hour night shifts. I had taken my first day off, so I only had to work one day shift and two nights. There was almost twelve hours between my last day shift and first night shift, so I could get Nikolas to daycare, head to the hospital and then straight to work for my night shift starting at 6pm.

Danika had a restless day as I sat with her. Helen had gone home for a bit to see Nikolas and to clear her head, get some fresh air, and just get out of the hospital and that awful isolation room. I was starting to see how exhausted Helen was from her hospital sojourn, but hopefully things would start to look up, although I was having thoughts about Danika not surviving this virus. Performing CPR on that little guy had sucked the life out me. I felt awful and had absolutely no energy.

Helen came back to the hospital at 3:30 pm, and I hung around until 4:00 before heading back to the firehouse. On the drive there I felt like I had the flu. A flu without aching bones or fever, just bagged. We were getting Critical

Incident Stress (CIS) counselling for yesterday's call which was something our department did after every death call.

I arrived about thirty minutes before shift change and went on a call immediately — a 'short of breath' for a 75-year-old smoker. I stormed off the truck thinking that this guy probably smokes two packs a day — no wonder he can't catch his breath. I was in a nasty mood. No empathy from me that shift. I was pissed at the world.

We went from that call straight to a Motor Vehicle Incident (MVI), and then finally got back to the firehouse two hours later.

I asked Captain Wally, "I'm feeling pretty crappy, do you mind if I don't eat, just lie on the couch?" He said it was cool, and I had lain there for barely fifteen minutes before we got the call for a 'struck cyclist'.

When we arrived, we could see a bike jammed under a vehicle. We hopped out of the rig and I noticed a kid sitting in the back of the car. He had some scrapes, and we gave him some oxygen because he looked a little shaky. We started to drive back to firehouse when Roger, checking around in the back, exclaimed: "Oh shit! We're out of O2 masks."

"Don't worry about it", I said, "we have tons back at the firehouse." As soon as I spoke, we were dispatched to an MVI that was very close to the firehouse, arriving in under a minute.

There were at least ten police cars already on the scene, and about fifty people standing around. When I opened the rig door, everyone was screaming. This is the most important time of any call. A firefighter must slow down, be composed and assess the situation, and most importantly stay calm. There was an over-turned Ford SUV in the road, a car pushed around a pole, and a woman screaming for help. The police cars still had their sirens on.

It was total chaos.

Roger went one way, and I went another, trying to ignore the screaming woman as I could see a guy on the ground further down the block. I started to run when another screaming woman finally got my attention. Behind her, on the bank beside the road, was a girl, face-down.

I moved down to her. I asked if this was her daughter. The woman just screamed louder without answering. The girl wasn't breathing. Looking for Roger, who was about one hundred feet away, I shouted at him to get me the bag valve mask so I could ventilate her. I did 'C' spine as I waited for him to bring me the equipment. We rolled her supine, supporting her head in line with her body as we moved her, in case she had a broken neck. There were five patients lying on the road and Roger left me with her to breathe using the bag valve mask and continue monitoring her present pulse.

I asked the screaming woman to tell me what happened. "We got hit by a car!" she screeched, and I assumed they must have been walking and the little girl was a pedestrian.

I looked back. There were several victims, so I wasn't getting any help. I checked her pulse as I was pumping oxygen into her lungs and now it was gone. I yelled to the captain that I needed help to do CPR while Engine 11 pulled up on scene along with the ambulance. I checked again, she had a pulse, so I decided to maintain holding her head as still as possible, beginning to ventilate her.

After a few short minutes, the paramedics brought a spine board and told me to keep bagging her and they would start CPR in the ambulance.

We got her onto the spine board and then the girl started to vomit everywhere — a very bad sign — and the paramedic yelled for his buddy. "We've got to take this one to Royal Columbian!" – A major trauma hospital in greater Vancouver. Rolling her gently and clearing the puke out of her airway, we got her onto a board and into the ambulance. I hopped in with them and we started moving right away.

I ventilated her while the paramedic started an IV drip. She kept puking everywhere, and we were using suction to clear her airway. The paramedic started asking me for info: how long was she down, what happened, how old, and a lot of other things I didn't know, so I replied I had no idea what happened. We drove, lights and siren, for about 10 minutes when I yelled that her pulse was gone. Her heart stopped. Now we had to initiate chest compressions.

The ambulance started to pull over. I asked what we were doing and was told advanced life support paramedics were meeting us and taking over. We stopped and switched personnel, but I stayed in the ambulance. As soon as the new paramedic got in, we started driving with full-on lights and siren. We drove past our city's major hospital, heading to Royal Columbian, the same place I had driven my daughter, and at that moment I knew the little girl had died.

Pulling up to the emergency entrance, there was very little talking in the ambulance. They had doctors waiting. Taking over the ventilations from me, they whisked her away into the trauma unit. Covered in blood, grass, and puke, I thought, *Wow, that was fucking crazy!*

Before calling a cab, I decided to take a pause and lie down near the ambulance. It was suddenly nice and quiet. I was flat on my back looking up at the stars when a paramedic walked up and said, "Hey buddy, you need a ride?" I told him I couldn't. I had to go back to Surrey and was supposed to go in a cab. He was heading back to the scene I just came from, right by my firehouse — so I thought *to hell with it* and hopped in with them. These were specialized infant transport team paramedics, the guys who pilot the Life Flight helicopter. He said they came to meet our ambulance carrying the little girl. They wanted to take her to Children's Hospital. There was no place like it, they said. I suddenly remembered Danika was there in isolation.

Holy crap, I forgot all about her! I took out my cell phone and called Helen. "She's really sick," said Helen.

I started freaking out and asked if I should come in, but Helen said no, that she would call me if anything happened. She asked how my night was going. I told her the firehouse had calls all night long, and I would tell her about it tomorrow. I said good night, and sitting in the ambulance, burst into tears. The paramedic in the passenger seat turned around and said, "You okay buddy?" I answered, "Yup." He turned back around.

When we arrived back at the accident, there were more police and news cameras than on a movie shoot. It was all lit up with investigators everywhere. When I stepped out of the ambulance a reporter I knew said, "Hey, Steve, did she make it?"

I said, "Sorry, don't know," but the reporter pressed, "Some of your co-workers said she was dead before they took her to the hospital?"

"She wasn't dead when she left," I told him.

"Did she survive?" He asked again. I trusted this guy, as he had been around our department longer than I had been and had a great reputation with the guys.

I shook my head and said, "Don't run it, but it did not look good when I left the hospital."

My engine was still at the scene, and the guys were almost ready to go, so my timing was perfect. I said goodbye to the paramedics and hopped on the rig. It was almost midnight then, and we hadn't eaten a thing, but I wasn't hungry at all. I just wanted to go to bed when we got to the firehouse. The captain asked if I was okay. He could see I was shivering though it wasn't cold. Maybe I was coming down with something, I thought.

Captain Wally started to explain what had happened in the accident. I thought the girl I attended was a pedestrian, but he explained she was in the Ford SUV when it was hit by a stolen car the police were chasing. That's why there were so many police cars at the scene. He said the SUV must have rolled two or three times and she was thrown out of the car because she wasn't wearing a seat belt.

Back at the firehouse, we got all the medical stuff back together, went over the engine from front-to-back, making sure it was ready for the next call. I'd only been a firefighter for ten years, but I'd been to so many calls where everything is not back on the rig, and you always seem to need that *one thing* you were missing. It's an important job to make sure the truck and equipment are back together. We are well trained to know exactly what is supposed to be there and where it goes. The craziest thing was I could not remember what was supposed to be in the medical bag. I have filled that thing hundreds of times in my career and now I was completely blank. I was still shivering.

I went up and showered, put on a new uniform, and came back downstairs to go over the call. That was something else Wally was big on: going over everything so we can learn from our mistakes and improve for the next time. I really liked that about Wally — no one could ever accuse him of not being thorough. He was always trying to do his best and I really respected him as a captain.

I found out the girl died at the hospital. She was eleven years old. She wasn't wearing her seatbelt.

It was a huge string of bad luck: a family driving home when a car being chased by the police *just happens* to run a stop sign at the same intersection they were driving through and, the saddest part of all, they *just happen* to hit a car with a girl inside not wearing her seatbelt. Her little five-year-old brother was sitting in the middle, wearing a seatbelt, but without a booster seat, and miraculously was unhurt. That's one of the things that pissed me off most about the job: the parents who are too busy to do the simple things and it cost them their kids. What a waste of a fucking life!

A cop by the name of Sandy (the firehouse knew her well) pulled over a suspicious looking Mustang. As she walked back to her patrol car, the driver took off. Just as she jumped into her cruiser, the Mustang hit the SUV at the next intersection. When we arrived on-scene, both of the pricks who stole the car were lying close to the young girl I attended. The entire scene was a mess, and it wasn't until Wally's debriefing that I could make sense of it. I went to bed feeling exhausted and still shaking, but in less than fifteen minutes the tone went. It was the start of a seven-call night.

I never did get to sleep that night, instead making do with two more showers from blood exposure during the calls on the rest of that hellish shift. There was one full arrest where Roger and I did fifteen straight minutes of CPR; then, a nasty MVI where we spent an hour trying to stop fluids from running down the storm sewers; then, a couple more 'nothing' calls; one false alarm; and then the shift was over. I drove home to see Nikolas and then headed straight to the hospital. I drank two cups of coffee but still had not eaten anything. I felt like shit.

Danika was sick with a very high fever, and terrible congestion. I was seriously terrified we were going to lose her. Helen paused her vigil to go down and get a coffee. I made sure not to tell Helen the kind of night I'd had, but I think she figured it out when she found me sound asleep in the chair two hours later.

I had been on the job ten years and had *never* called in sick, but I was debating on doing it for the last night shift. The day before, my battalion chief had pulled me aside to ask me if I needed anything, to just let him know. It meant a ton to me. He'd always been understanding. I didn't feel great but also didn't want to look like I couldn't take it. I decided to do my last night shift because we had the CIS counselling planned for that night. One last night, I figured. I will do it, and then be more than glad to have my four days off.

Heading to work, from the hospital, I stopped for a red light and started crying. I was crying and shaking like never before. I put on my sunglasses so no one in the cars beside me would notice. I must have cried for thirty minutes straight, and then felt completely fine, arriving at the firehouse my usual thirty minutes before the shift at 5:30 pm.

The battalion chief had taken all three crews out of service so we could be debriefed together. RCMP officer Sandy (who had given chase to the stolen car) was also there. She looked like hell, but so did the rest of us. These CIS counselling sessions could be helpful sometimes. I am a big believer in going through those sessions as a crew, but I was just not ready that night.

The session started with Sandy telling us she had seen the 16-year-old in jail, the one who stole the car, and told him that he killed an 11-year-old girl.

He answered, "So? Shit happens."

I was ready to explode when she said that. There were fifteen people in the room, and everyone had to express how they felt. Two firefighters had dealt with the prick who stole the car, and said he was screaming and abusive.

When they got to me the facilitator said, "So Steve, tell us how you are feeling." As soon I heard that, I felt like bursting out crying. *Oh my God*, I thought, *get a hold of yourself.*

"Steve, are you able to tell us how you are feeling?" he repeated.

It seemed like five minutes, but was only thirty or forty seconds, before I calmly said,

"Now that I have all the information, and I know the guy who stole that car was just a few feet away, I wish I had walked over, picked up a massive rock, and dropped it on his head."

It wasn't exactly what I wanted to say, or exactly how I wanted to say it, but it was close. *Fuck it,* I thought, neither in a good mood nor interested in being there. I didn't get asked to say any more and the questioning moved to the firefighter beside me.

It took two and a half hours to say our peace and the rigs were released back into service. We ate dinner at about 10:30 pm and I went straight to bed.

We only had two calls, but by 5:30 am, I wasn't sleeping. I lay in my bed crying for an hour. Sure enough, at 6:10 am the tone went off:

"Engine 10, Engine 10, call for an infant in distress." *You have to be fucking kidding me*, I thought. *Not again.*

I ran down the hall, still emotional, with tears rolling down my face. Grabbing my bunker gear, I hopped on the truck, still throwing it on as we were rolling onto the street.

We arrived to find a woman high on crack and her baby in full arrest on the floor. This child was two months old. We started CPR. The mom, after loading up on crack, had been breastfeeding when she passed out. The little baby girl had rolled off her lap and suffocated in-between the cushions and the back of the leather couch. I was a walking disaster and couldn't believe this was happening. If my own baby daughter had not been in the hospital, possibly dying, maybe I could have dealt with it all better.

We could not revive this baby girl. She had been down way too long and likely died hours ago. Dickhead paramedic and his partner didn't show, thank God. I would have hammered him for sure! In reality, the guy was a black belt in Taekwondo and would have kicked my ass, I'm sure. But I would've felt better if I could hit him just *once*, for the three dead kids, and for my daughter. I had never before had three dead kids in four days, combined with my own daughter slowly passing away in the hospital.

We got back to firehouse late, ten minutes past our regular shift change at 8:00 am and the other crew was waiting. I was soaked through with sweat and had to shower again before heading off to see Nikolas, and then to the hospital. Nikolas was great to see, so beautiful with his Woody and Buzz Lightyear dolls.

"Hi Dada," he screamed when he saw me. I started to cry when he jumped into my arms, and I squeezed him hard.

What the hell is wrong with me? I am a mess—enough of this crying stuff, I thought. I hugged him until Kath, our daycare friend, said jokingly,

"Okay Steve, let him go—you're gonna suffocate him!"

I freaked and shouted, "What?"

I was shaking.

Kath, a little nervous, placated me by saying, "It's time for Nikolas to eat."

As I was leaving, Kath asked if I was okay. I told her I was sorry, and that it had been a long night. She was an awesome friend, ran a great daycare, and when it came to Nikolas, went above and beyond for Helen and me.

Driving to the hospital, I talked out loud: "No more crying, I'm good now. I need to be strong for Danika and Helen." I cranked the tunes and tried to sing, but that didn't work either.

I couldn't get past my rage for Dickhead the paramedic who responded to my daughter; for the mom who didn't put her son in a booster, or tell her

---

daughter to put on her fucking seatbelt. I felt numb about the two babies who had suffocated to death. I couldn't rationalize those calls. I was over-thinking and taking everything personally.

I arrived at the hospital, shaking or shivering, adrenaline racing through my body. I picked up an extra-large coffee because on top of everything else, I felt bad for falling asleep the day before with Danika in isolation and did not want to do it again.

Danika was the same as yesterday, feverish and very sick. Helen asked why I didn't call, and I replied again, "Long night." We had been together long enough for Helen to know not to question me further when I answered like that.

Of course, I didn't tell her that on that last hellish shift, I'd completely forgotten about Danika — not to mention Helen. I convinced her to go home to spend some time with Nikolas. She was gone for most of the day, and this time I managed to stay awake. She came back around 8:00 pm and I went home.

I picked up Nikolas, Buzz Lightyear and Woody, and put them all in his little plastic tyke bed. I slept on the floor beside him. I needed to be there with him. I slept really well, even though I had a crazy nightmare. But I have nightmares all the time, sometimes waking up yelling or standing on the bed. When we first got married, it freaked Helen out, but she's used to it now. In the morning, we got up and both had a bowl of Lucky Charms for breakfast. Then, as per our routine, I took Nikolas next door to Kath's, and drove to the hospital.

On day nine, Danika's fever broke. The doctor met with us and Helen asked if we could take Danika home. If she was not going to be intubated, we could manage her ourselves and return to the hospital if the fever came back. The doctor said fever was a major concern but to our surprise, agreed, because it appeared Danika was improving, and Helen was a nurse. By day eleven, the fever returned. We had a bag packed at the front door in case we had to make a speedy run to the hospital.

I switched my holidays with another firefighter. I now had twelve days off, giving me time to be with my family. I'd been feeling exhausted—mentally and physically—since that last shift and the continual underlying worry about our baby girl.

Come day sixteen, Danika was back in Children's, but this time they told us she was going to be okay. The doctor explained she had scarring on her esophagus and lungs and would most likely have bad asthma, but the next few months and coming years would tell them how much actual damage was done. We were alright with all that. What else could we do? Helen and I took her home to recover.

Although I felt tremendously relieved that little Danika's life was saved, I felt like the world had slowed down and I was swimming through molasses. I could not seem to concentrate. Mostly when I was driving by myself or lying in bed, waves of sadness and crying would just come out of nowhere.

I took up self-medication in hopes it would help me sleep. Pounding back three or four rum and Cokes before bed helped me relax for sure, but several nights I would wake up multiple times covered in sweat. I know many first responders feel this way after traumatic calls and usually with time, associated negative thoughts will dissipate. They always did for me in the past. This time was different. Never before had I experienced constant crying spells and felt such sadness. All I wanted was to stop thinking about the calls.

CHAPTER TWO

Tell Me a Little About Yourself

The first few days I was off the job I didn't contact anyone in the department. I was trying to clear my head by forgetting about work. The next week, some of the guys from my immediate crew called to see if we needed anything — if there was something they could do.

Apparently, a rumour was going around the department that my daughter had passed away. We received flowers and a card from the fire chief, which read: 'Our condolences for the loss of your daughter.' I phoned the battalion chief's office and told them that Danika was still with us — she had not died — and I'd appreciate the rumour being quashed. Rumours spread quickly in a fire department with several hundred people employed across fifteen halls.

Another call came asking me to attend a second CIS debriefing because the incident where the eleven-year-old died was all over the news. The family was furious at the police for creating a high-speed chase that killed their little girl. This was bullshit. Not only had the cop pulled the car over, it then only accelerated for one block. If that little girl had her seatbelt on, she would be alive. I believed the parents were at fault. At the same time, I understood that if I had lost *my* kid, I would want to put the blame on someone else.

I did *not* want to go to that stress debriefing. I was still furious, not ready to talk. I knew the policy would request that I see a shrink, and I was not ready for that trial either.

Captain Wally called me the next day saying he wanted to talk to our CIS debriefing team on the following day. I said I wasn't ready. He understood, but said it was important for me to talk to someone. There are eight CIS facilitators listed by the department and I could talk to any one of them.

I wasn't sleeping well — drinking was not giving me any relief — but I wasn't ready to talk yet. Helen was still in shock from everything that had happened over the last two weeks, and I sure as hell didn't want to bother her about not feeling well. She was, and is, amazing. She is always supportive when I'm off-kilter, *especially* after bad calls. She can spot it right away, giving me lots of space, and gently starting conversations. She also needed emotional support from me. We were both still worried about Danika even though she was home again and gradually recovering.

Two weeks later, I returned to work for my four days on. The guys on the crew called me a zombie. I wasn't engaging or talking much. I don't remember the four days or any specific calls. Waves of emotion would wash over me. I found myself crying on the way home and at night. I had hot flashes and nausea.

The battalion chief got word that I didn't look right and showed up on my last night shift. We talked for about an hour until a structure fire call came in and he had to split.

Over the last decade, I had seen a psychologist twice after bad calls. It did nothing for me. And both those psychologists I went to see wanted to talk about my childhood, asking if I was having (or ever had) suicidal thoughts, and so on. The problem with me seeing psychologists was that I didn't want to talk about my childhood, which they never seemed to understand. If I didn't feel a connection, chatting with someone who is getting paid to talk just doesn't work for me.

I knew I was in a bad way. With pressure from some of the guys at work, and Helen saying she had never seen me like this before, I was caught off guard. I thought I was hiding it well, at least from Helen. I agreed to see a counsellor and pulled a random name off my Critical Incident Stress card. I called Karie and told her I was going in.

I went to see a counsellor by the name of Tim. The first session was just a waste of time. I couldn't engage, I felt tired, explaining away that I would be better at the next session.

I worked another four days before Wally told me, again, that he was sincerely worried about me, that he could tell I wasn't right. I lied. I told him I had been going to counselling and that Danika had not been sleeping well, that I was tired from being up all night, but was actually feeling a little better. He let it go. The truth was that I felt like shit, and people seemed to moving and talking in slow motion. It was so weird.

Helen also told me that she was worried, and I lied to her as well. I told her that my first session with the counsellor was great but the guys on the crew kept talking about the calls, and it was draining me a bit. I told Helen we were almost done talking over the graphic calls, and promised her I would bounce right back. She reluctantly said *okay*. Of course, Helen knew exactly what was going on, but she gave me the space to sort things out. I had been playing hockey three times a week but had not gone out once in the last month. I had no energy. Now, lying to people I loved, it felt like I was on an island. I knew I needed to find the right counsellor to get back on track. I was, finally, ready to get better but I never went back to see Tim.

A few days later, I was waiting outside the White Rock office of another CIS-referred psychologist named Bill. When he asked me to come in and sit down, ten minutes late, I knew the routine. I was used to this part of therapy—the meeting with questions I didn't like, then deciding that it wasn't working for me.

"So, how are you doing?" Bill asked.

"Alright," I said.

"How *is* the fire department these days?" As a referral psychologist, Bill had seen tons of firefighters and likely heard it all.

The funny thing about being a firefighter is that everyone thinks it is dangerous. It isn't, not really. We are extremely well trained and have such state-of-the-art equipment that we can handle almost anything. The problem with my department was the new fire chief. I thought he was an asshole —trying to change our shifts to eight hours and reducing staffing by bringing in two-person fire trucks with remote control nozzles and pump panels. It can't be easy being in charge of hundreds of firefighters but to take a new job and try to change the world at the same time is just plain stupid.

So I started my ramble, telling Bill everything he already knew.

"Have you heard about our new two-man fire trucks, the quick response vehicles?"

"I actually live in Surrey," he predictably replied, "and have several fire-fighters as clients."

Yeah whatever, I'm thinking, already not liking this guy. *He's full of himself.* Plus, he was ten minutes late. Because I supposedly needed this guy's help, I drove all the way down to his office, and he showed up late. Again, this was not my first rodeo, and I quickly knew whether or not the session was going to be helpful. This is the kind of guy who will let me ramble for half an hour and then ask, without referring to anything I've said, "So tell me about your childhood."

"What is it that bothers you about those trucks?" Bill asked.

God, I thought again, *it's going to be a long hour.*

The local Workers Safety Act states that we must enter a burning building with no less than two guys going in and two guys at the doorway on standby to do rescue. We had several occasions where those QR's (quick response vehicles), had been on scene first — when they would typically have to do a search — but the second rig is ten minutes away. So, by law, they are supposed to wait while the house, apartment or commercial building burns away, and tell the mother, neighbour, or owner, "It's okay, another firetruck will be here shortly, and then we will go get your kid, wife, whatever."

Of course, no one waits — crews have gone in early even for a dog, because that is what we do. We are trained for the first couple of years to be able to deal with nearly every situation, but of course, you can't train for every single thing. When that tone goes off, you become robotic, instantly charged, and ready to go. Ninety-nine percent of all firefighters' and cops' training kicks in when they need it. That is what all the training does and is supposed to do — we don't care if it's not safe or what the law says. A kid could be trapped in a burning house and inevitably die if you don't go in there right away. We go in.

So how does it feel when you're fully trained, you know your shit and you can do a pretty damn good job, but some dumbass wet-behind-the-ears fire chief comes along and shakes things up because they need to save some money? Did I mention this new fire chief gets a bonus package? Ten per-cent, or ten bucks for every hundred he shaves off the current operating costs. My whole rant to Bill turns into how we won't get hurt, but the public hates us when we look like a bunch of idiots following the new protocol. The one comment that every firefighter and police officer has heard a million times is, "We pay your wages."

By now, Bill is coming across as a tad bored. He gets into the standard stuff with, "So, Steve, why are you here to see me?"

"I had three bad calls in a matter of four days," I replied.

"How many calls do you do on a shift?" he asked.

I quickly shot back, "On a crazy day my rig can do over twenty calls and on a slow shift, three to five."

He could hear by my cocky tone I was beginning to get frustrated. He wasn't impressed. To tell the truth, I was a little afraid of how I'd been feeling, so I wanted this guy to help me, but I just couldn't feel it. Helen thought it best for the whole family that I seek help. *So help me!* I wanted to scream. I reset and came clean with Bill in my sincerest voice.

"Listen — I'm here because I realize I'm depressed, but I struggle with going to these sessions. It's really hard for me to open up in this setting." I continued on, "Since that last crappy set of calls, and my daughter Danika getting really sick, I haven't wanted to go back to work. The last couple of years have been hard on my family. My brother became suicidal and I spent the last few years with him in and out of addiction facilities, and then one day he gave up on life and was gone. I feel partially responsible for the loss of my brother … there was a ton of shit going on there for a while and I'm still in the dumps."

"Please, *explain* to me how you are feeling. What do you mean, in the dumps?" Bill retorted without looking up. *Behind his little castle desk, he's probably looking at porn*, I'm thinking. My God, this guy was brutal — only a few minutes in and I've spilled my guts and he didn't even look up. At that moment I hated him and the session. I stuck it out though, since I had promised Helen.

"Well, I've never had this happen before, but … I don't want to get out of bed …."

I tried to explain.

"I just have no desire to start the day… and no wish to go back to work tomorrow. I've been a firefighter for over ten years, love my job … not every minute, but most of the time … but, for whatever reason, I suddenly don't want to do it anymore."

Once it started to pour out, I could not rein it back in.

"I'm drinking tons more. One-a-day isn't the average anymore. I pound back vodka and rum every day of the week now. I lie in bed until noon on days when I can. To be honest, there's no desire to get out of bed … it's weird. I'll wake up multiple times from nightmares, force myself to go back to sleep, but wake up again the same way in an hour and then lie there, exhausted. I have an awesome wife, a great son, and a new baby girl … but something is *wrong*. I try and force myself to be happy about everything, but it doesn't work. Even when I manage to get going out the door, I dread the rest of the day … dread everything … a weird feeling … like my life has no meaning. I had this feeling back when I was a kid, and I didn't want to live."

Oops. That's the wrong thing to say to a psychologist.

"Are you having suicidal thoughts now?" Bill asked.

I quickly shot back, "No."

"Have you ever had thoughts of wanting to kill yourself?"

Oh, I wish I didn't say that … that I didn't want to live. I knew the next by-the-book shrink question was: 'Tell me about your childhood,' so I dove into that bit myself, not wanting to waste any more of Bill's precious session time.

"Honestly, have you ever treated anyone who hasn't had suicidal thoughts?" I asked, trying to laugh it off. Yet again, Billy-boy wasn't too impressed. If he was disappointed with my

question to him, I didn't really care. We were both burning the hour, now.

"So, would you say you had a *happy* childhood?"

I was incensed, "Come on, are you fucking kidding me?" *He was going through the motions, picking the low-hanging fruit … well, I'm here … what the hell, I'll answer.*

"Once, when I was in high school, I thought about killing myself. I'm still not sure if I would've had the balls to do it — well, obviously not. I'm still here. What I mean is … one day back then, I was feeling a little bit like I am right now … like no one understands me."

"Tell me about your first day of high school," Bill said.

"Okay," I said. "The first day, I was walking home with a new friend and a large group of teens blocked my path. As I tried to get by, three guys pulled me into the crowd and started punching me. I decided to turtle on the ground until they stopped, but they started kicking me, so I jumped to my feet to run from them. I got a few hundred yards when one of the guys caught up and started punching me again and calling me a loser. I started crying and saw them all laughing at me. I had a fight with his younger brother during the summer, and this was pay back for that. The problem was the huge group of kids seeing me get beat — crying and running like a scared dog. How would I ever shake that reputation?

"I went home and lay on the kitchen floor and decided that I could never go back to that school again. I felt I was so fucked! I was having trouble breathing, one of my ribs was really hurting me and I just hated my life, and I would be known at high school as that loser who got the shit kicked out of him, and the cry baby. I just *felt* like killing myself but I didn't. So I guess I wasn't really suicidal."

"How did you feel, in the weeks and months after that day?" Bill asked.

"I felt sorry for myself but had felt that way for years before because of my family and home life. That beating I took on the first day seemed to bring everything to the surface. High school was hard. Those guys tormented me daily and I was very aware that there could be a possible beating right around the corner. I got used to being punched in the head or gut as they passed me in the hall or made threats off the school grounds. After my father put me in boxing, I realized, no matter how bad life was or how crappy I felt, I *wanted to live*."

Bill moved on, "Were your parents always supportive of you and your brother and sister?"

I wanted to walk over and slap him across the head. *That's such a fucking stupid question*, I thought. *Who the hell can honestly say their parents were always there for them?*

"Both my parents worked their asses off, but they were big drinkers and that screwed everything up," I said.

"You saw your parents drunk a lot?"

"My mom would be staggering drunk no less than five times a week, if not every day. My dad would down between five and ten drinks a day — even more, when my mom got loaded, probably because it eased his pain. Hah! They were awesome people, just brutal role models."

"Did you feel angry about it?"

"Not now, but at the time, I felt sorry for myself, to be honest. I used to fight a lot in elementary school. Guidance counsellors loved to tell me that this was an obvious release of aggression."

"Did you enjoy the fighting?"

"Actually, I did. I wasn't a very good fighter, winning less than half. For some reason kids always challenged me, and I didn't care if I won or lost. The stakes were low — you only got bruised — I never got badly hurt and it released so much tension out of my system. I guess it worked for me."

"Are you thinking about hurting yourself or taking your own life right now?"

As soon as I got into answering his questions, he would go onto the next one, like he didn't give a shit about what I had just said. I was choking up, but he didn't seem to notice.

"No," I answered. The truth was, I was having some pretty dark thoughts, as most first responders do after traumatic events, but not about taking my own life. Now I was just feeling depressed.

Bill looked at his watch and said: "Well, Steve, we've made a bit of progress. I think by wanting to live, you've built in a mechanism that turns you around when you get low. I'm not worried about the way you talk about your feelings — you have a good grasp on your thoughts — but you have definitely had mental trauma in your life. The way you are feeling is not uncommon with first responders, or people who have been to war."

Blah, blah, blah ... I thought, *tell me something I don't know.*

"I would like to see you again next week."

He suggested that I think back and document some of the calls that may have affected me. *Are you fucking kidding? Every single call has affected me, that's why I came.* I didn't need to think back, the calls were already in the front of my mind — I was reliving them as if I'd attended them yesterday.

I cancelled my second appointment with Bill. I never went to see him again. He was one of the reasons first responders don't seek help. There are so many clowns like Bill out there making money from struggling cops, firefighters, and paramedics with no understanding of how to really have a conversation with them.

I returned to work not feeling any better. Once you start the counselling process, no one checks back with you to ask how it went because of privacy issues. It is a major flaw in the system. I just told people I was still going. Helen, however, knew I wasn't. She was worried and wanted me to find someone else.

That feverless flu feeling continued to kill any energy I had, and dark thoughts still rattled around in my head. I felt awful. I ended up calling a friend who had been through a ton of stuff and asked him for advice. Pete was very experienced, the union leader of Surrey Fire, who later went on to hold the ranking of sixth District President of the International Association of Firefighters. A higher-up for certain, but he'd always told me he would be there to listen — a great guy overall, with time for everyone.

Pete said he liked what the psychologist had suggested —it might be time to revisit those bad calls. He called it 'duffle bag syndrome' when the bag fills up and starts to overflow. Peter thought my duffle bag was overflowing and I needed to empty some of it. I respected Pete. He was a very smart guy and I listened to him carefully. He said that shrinks want to go back into someone's childhood because that is always where the issues begin. Pete laughed and said, "I know a lot about you Steve — in fact, I know you better than you know."

We both laughed, but he was serious, saying, "I'm sorry, but your childhood is fucked up, man — you really need to take this shit seriously— especially the way you are feeling."

Pete asked me if I had ever heard of PTSD (Post-Traumatic Stress Disorder), and I said honestly, I hadn't. He explained that guys coming back from the wars in Vietnam and the Middle East had this stress syndrome that took over their lives and drove many of them to suicide. He said that they were looking into it for firefighters — there was some real evidence linking PTSD to multiple or repeated traumatic calls — and guys like me could be suffering from it.

Pete wanted me to see Teresa, a psychologist based in New Westminster. He had heard good things about her practice, and called on my behalf, 'knowing me better than I know myself.' *Maybe he should go see her*, I thought, *and come back and tell me what to do*. Again, it was the first time I'd ever heard of PTSD, but I did know something was deeply wrong with me. I decided to take Pete's advice and try again with his favoured psychologist.

The office was in an old storefront, in an old part of town, so parking was a nightmare. Unlike Bill, Teresa was ready for me right on time. She gave me a cup of tea and set about making me feel comfortable, asking if there was anything I needed help with right now.

I had a really good vibe sitting there sipping my tea.

I answered yes, I needed help with the dark thoughts and the nightmares I was having. She wrote something down and asked, "Would you like to learn a trick to help you with that, how to block your thoughts?" Firefighters love short cuts and tricks, and I immediately answered yes.

"Okay then, first tell me a bit about yourself," Teresa said.

I told her briefly about losing my brother to addiction and mental illness and how he had recently taken his own life. I spoke about my daughter catching the deadly RSV virus, and me responding to three kid deaths in four days. I told her I had no energy and was having dark thoughts, weird dreams, and drinking heavily.

Teresa looked genuinely concerned as I was speaking, and for the first time it felt like someone was actually listening.

"Steve", she said, "we are going to start with your sleep, because without adequate sleep and proper REM sleep, it is difficult to recover from the trauma you have just been through. There is a technique I use with police, firefighters and paramedics that is helpful in assisting the mind to shut down unwanted thoughts."

I smiled and said, "Okay, you got me, what is it?"

Without missing a beat, Teresa told me to close my eyes and tell her what a stop sign looked like in detail. I described it as red with white letters and a white border around the octagon shape. Then, she asked me to draw it on a flip chart pad. With a red marker, I replicated it to actual size.

When I was finished, she ripped it off, gave to me and said, "Every time the thoughts come into your head, think of that stop sign. Over time, the thoughts will fade away." Then she cautioned, "It will take some work to control those thoughts."

Teresa explained that our first visit was meant to be a casual meeting. We would talk and get to know each other a little. Aside from the immediate simple stop sign trick, if I was interested, she would give me a project when I left. I felt very comfortable with her, drinking tea and talking about the weather. We didn't just talk about me either. Teresa told me about her life, her kids, and how much she loved helping people. It was comforting, speaking with her.

She was very big on letting her patients dictate the sessions and asked, "Steve, what do you want to talk about? What do you not want to discuss?"

"I think I somehow made a connection between the death of those two infants and the little girl to my daughter who was deathly ill in the hospital, and it caused some kind of chemical reaction, making me feel sick and have nightmares." Teresa was writing stuff down and I kept talking, "I feel that part is what I need to focus on. I had pretty well made peace with losing my brother."

Teresa asked what the details were surrounding his death and I said that he took his own life. He told me he was going do it and he did, it was pretty simple. I said I didn't really want to say any more about him right now but would let her know when I felt comfortable talking about his death.

"No problem. I am here to support you in any way I can."

Wow, what a relief to hear that. As I finished my tea, Teresa continued writing and said, "I am really glad we were able to meet and am looking forward to working with you. I have noted not to ask questions about your brother or his death."

"Thank you," I said.

She asked how I was feeling about my first visit. I said, "I am very comfortable, much to my surprise."

"Why is that?"

"Well just like that, not having to talk about my brother — I like the way you handled that. The other thing I don't like about going to counselling is I'm usually asked about my childhood as soon I sit down."

Teresa explained how it is hard to help someone if they don't want to talk about the things that are bothering them. Childhood traumatic events that are remembered and not repressed are not just important to the health professional, but critical for patient healing and recovery of mental health.

It totally made sense, but I said, "I struggle about things in my childhood … I'm not sure I can talk about them."

"Steve, how about we start small and go from there? At any time, if you don't want to talk about something, we can move past it."

I liked that idea. When the session was ending, Teresa said she would like me to go home and write a short story about my childhood right up to the end of high school. She asked me for one favour: "Don't block memories if they start pouring out. Keep writing. Even if you don't want to talk about it, there is a benefit to writing your thoughts down and reflecting on them."

She gave me a little worksheet with questions to get me started. She said I might never need to see a psychologist again if I learned how to channel my thoughts properly. Teresa thought it would be easy for me once I understood the process. She knew I would like that statement, and to be honest I really felt okay going back into my childhood with her. I am not proud of my past, but I was sure I could open up and face it with Teresa's help.

As I was leaving, Teresa told me she already had a good feeling about who I was as a person, and that she understood why I was having nightmares and uncontrollable thoughts. She insisted that I get physically active again, doing whatever I wanted to get my heart rate up and feel tired afterward. I liked her and promised I would do my best to work hard and not disappoint her. I really wanted to feel better. She told me to come back anytime I thought I needed to speak with her.

Teresa had left the ball in my court as to whether or not I wanted to see her again. That was a plan I was happy to follow. You see, first responders need to feel supported, not told what to do, but to be asked instead. So I went away and started writing shit down about my life as far back as I can remember and right up to the present. I was determined to unload the duffle bag and think clearly again. I felt sure that writing my story would finally shake loose those nasty dark thoughts.

CHAPTER THREE

Born a Mistake

"You can't connect the dots looking forward; you can only connect them looking backwards. So you have to trust that the dots will somehow connect in your future. You have to trust something — your gut, destiny, life, karma, whatever."
– Steve Jobs

Hindsight may very well be 20/20, but for many of us, the bad memories of childhood trauma are something we want to hide — to ignore, to bury and move on. As adults, we just want to live a 'normal' life raising our own kids differently than we were raised. From a young age, you learn that crying doesn't help or change much of anything. Instead, you learn to deny and repress the bad memories. But the *hidden* has a way of coming back to bite you unexpectedly.

Either you find a way to deal with your past and grow from it, as a trauma counsellor advised me, or you can choose drugs to deal with it — but the depression and addiction will lead you to an early death if you choose the latter. A good counsellor can help you resurface from the deep and surprisingly, in the process of digging into your past, you will unearth good memories too. To know who you are is a liberating discovery.

Growing up, I was the little shit in the neighbourhood. When something went missing in my neighbourhood, everyone pointed to me, and in most cases, they were right. If you turned on the Christmas lights in your yard, and one night there were none — not one bulb to be had —it was me. I didn't take them to sell or even smash. Just the act of stealing them did something for me, which I can't really explain. Adults would say it was 'acting out' but I just remember being a kid doing bad things for most of my childhood. As I got older, I did do some good but I don't remember those things as much. I have flashbacks all the time of doing something bad, like stealing something. And now as an adult, I feel ashamed.

Looking back, one of the first events I remember was breaking my leg just after my fifth birthday. Snow hit the ground in November 1969, and my father, an avid skier, took me up to Mount Seymour, the local ski mountain. We headed up to the top of a small hill called Goldie.

A push and a shove from my Dad sent me flying down the hill. Right away, my left ski crossed over the other, but the binding didn't pop, and there was a loud *crack*. My fibula and tibia broke above the boot in several places — so much for soft bones. My father came running, picked me up with my skis on and carried me down to the car. I remember, to this day, screaming, throwing up, and then feeling very tired and sleeping most of the drive — a full hour, in a blizzard, to Vancouver General Hospital. I woke up to a jello cup after surgery. I was only there for three days, but it felt like months. I hated that stay, the room, the smell, and the staff. I still don't like hospitals, and I'm pretty sure that experience is the reason.

For years, I didn't want to think about my childhood but remembering and writing it down is for me far easier than talking about it. It's a slow process that gradually allows one memory after another to emerge and the dots to start connecting.

My family didn't look like your average family. I had a sister, Sonya, who was four years older than me. We did not get along very well when we were smaller, always fighting. Serious, *physical* fights. She handled me quite easily, but I was always pushing her buttons for more. I found out later in life that my father was forty-five years old when he had me. I asked him once what the hell he had been thinking.

"You were a mistake," he said. "You were conceived in a tent on a camping trip." Then he followed up with, "If it makes you feel any better, your sister was a mistake too!" Honestly, I did feel better.

I had a half-brother, from my mother's first marriage. Her husband was killed but the reason was never talked about. Greg had twelve years on me, long hair and was great with girls but kind of socially strange. I thought he was so cool. But he always told me my father didn't like him. There was some truth to that — I can't remember him and my dad laughing together or having fun, ever. I don't know what my brother was like when he was young. I only knew him as a teenager and that he made his own bed more often than not when it came to getting in trouble. Greg had parties, with lots of weed, in the basement of our house and that drove my old-fashioned European father *crazy*. My brother would freak out if anyone questioned him, and he was a big guy. He had several breakdowns and was always somewhat unstable. I remember three crazy things he did, and I'm sure a couple of them were just to piss off my dad.

When I was in kindergarten, he bought a monkey. Yup, some mongrel monkey that he kept in a cage in the basement. The monkey's name was Suzy, a half-breed with super sharp fangs who used to bite if you didn't comply with her wishes. Our entire house stank. The basement reeked of urine and feces because the monkey would throw it out of her cage. It was all over the walls and the floor, my brother never cleaned it up. My mom brought the monkey to school one day for show-and-tell when I was in grade one. I became the coolest kid for about a week because I had a monkey — that was the best part. The other great thing was that monkey *did not* like my sister. One time, it grabbed her hair and started going crazy, throwing her around the living room. I really enjoyed that show. Finally something beating up my sister! You know you are having it bad when you get the shit kicked out of you by a monkey. With her beating me up since I was little, I now had a monkey on my side. The worst part though — it was the dirtiest animal you could imagine, always so loud, shaking its cage all the time, and the shit everywhere.

After about eighteen months, Greg traded the monkey to someone for a two-foot-long baby alligator. The alligator lived its life in the basement bathtub. My brother used to bring it out of the tub, put rubber bands around its jaw, and walk it around the stinky basement Again, my father was furious but never said anything to my brother. In hindsight, it's obvious *why* they didn't have a great relationship. The one thing my brother had on his side was that he was a brilliant, straight-A student and the teachers loved him — the opposite of me.

One night my brother was arrested for fighting with a prostitute. At about three in the morning, the Vancouver Police called my dad. My brother's story was that he had been in a restaurant and for no reason at all a hooker came over and stabbed him. I never heard the true story, from either my brother or my father, but Greg ended up in the hospital with a stab wound and was charged with assault of some kind. Like I said, I didn't know my brother well, but to me he was always cool, always in some kind of trouble. But so was everybody in our neighbourhood. If you've ever seen the movie *Boogie Nights*, my brother's life was like a scene right out of that movie.

My father was a part-time janitor, part-time drywaller, and my mother worked on the canning line in a fishery. I grew up hanging out on Boundary Road which separated East Vancouver from Burnaby — a low-income area with lots of drugs and crime around. My parents struggled to make ends meet every month. There was never any extra money for anything.

Alcohol had a huge effect on my family. My father drank six beers nightly on a weekday and added a couple of whiskey shots and glasses of wine on the weekends. He was never slurring or staggering loaded, rather a kind of happy drunk. He was a good man and I loved him — he just liked his drink. My mom, on the other hand, was owned by the bottle. She worked long hours and drank straight vodka, usually killing a whole bottle a day. She was always staggering and mixed her vodka in milk, of all things, to hide it at times — she thought we couldn't smell it then. She never admitted drinking alcohol — always said she was on medication.

So, my earliest memories are that broken leg, scrapping with my sister, a monkey in the basement and an alligator in the tub, my brother getting stabbed by a prostitute, and my parents totally loaded and fighting all the time. Police were constantly responding to the house, and occasionally, someone would get taken away. For as long as I can remember, there was drinking, yelling, and stuff getting smashed.

My parents were good people though, hard-working laborers and the nicest souls you could ever meet when sober. When they were together, however, not so much. There was always drinking and fighting — a very negative environment when I look back on it now. My mother blamed my father for everything: her bad job, losing her hair, her varicose veins, and wrinkles. She brought her complaints up over and over when she drank.

In her younger years, my mother was a spectacular-looking woman — model-like, with the looks to go places. Louise Hansen, my mother, was born in Blenkinsop Bay just off Vancouver Island and raised with her brother and three sisters on Quadra Island. My grandparents made a homestead of one-hundred acres there in the early-to-mid 1900s after coming over from Norway. My mother was homeschooled, and the kids were left for weeks at a time while my grandparents went away to work in the logging camps. My mom would tell me stories of her childhood, and they sounded like such an amazing way to grow up — shooting guns, fishing — all without any rules.

I do have fond memories of my mother. She was the hardest worker you have ever seen, working lots of overtime followed by months of no work. The fish cannery lifestyle was not a good one. She used to take the bus to work at 5:00 am, pull a twelve-hour shift, then get off the bus halfway home to go to my Grandma's house, make her dinner and give her meds and then get back on the bus and come home. She would sometimes make us dinner late at night for the next day and drink in the few hours she had before bed. When I was in elementary school, she always had food on the table for my breakfast before she went to work. I remember when I was in grade one, my mom always left me toast and jam, and then call me at 8:00 am to wake me up. I would answer and immediately fall back to sleep and was pretty much late every day for a couple of years. It was only when the teacher said I would have to repeat grade two, if I didn't smarten up, that I started getting to school before the bell — at least fifty percent of the time.

My mother always took my side when she was sober. If I went to bed early enough and she wasn't drunk yet, she would come tuck me in and tell me a story. She told me about the dark nights on Quadra Island, when it was just her and a younger sister in the old five-bedroom house, with a gun, shooting at animals (or what they thought were animals) circling the home late at night. I loved hearing her stories, the few times that it happened. She was beautiful when she wasn't drinking.

My father was also a great guy who worked out of town for months at a time when I was young. Comparing my parent's childhoods, my father definitely had the tougher life. Bosko Serbedzija was my Dad's real name.

He was a Bosnian Serb who emigrated from the former Yugoslavia in the mid-1950s to Ontario to start a new life as a coal miner. His name, Bosko Serbedzija, was not ideal on job applications. My father was told to change it to improve his chances of getting work. After weeks of being rejected at the coal mine, my father walked in with his new name — Bob Serbic — and was hired on the spot.

My father's mother died when he was two years old. When he was a teenager, his father died in his arms after being shot when the German controlled Ustashe rolled into the villages in the area. He was a very angry young man. My father and a few of his friends became guerilla militia. They hid up in the hills and shot into the camps or the marching line of invading troops. As a child, I remember a scary looking man coming up to me in church one day to tell me my dad was a hero. He sat down and explained.

When a line of tanks and armored vehicles tried to come through a valley into another local village, my father and his friends held them off by shooting, then running, then shooting again. The scary man told me that to the troops, it looked like there were dozens of snipers, but in reality, there were only five. The village was able to load up their things and escape safely thanks to my father and his friends.

My father was reluctant to talk about those days, but he did tell me an incredible story of friendship. After the death of his mother, he was raised by his grandmother for most of his childhood. It was very important to her to feed him well, always making him a lunch. At his little school, there was a big Croatian kid who never had any food, so my father always gave him half of his sandwich. He said the kid never spoke, was very quiet, but always took the offered half.

Years later, after the war started and a couple of years into being a guerilla, my father and two of his friends were captured by the Germans. They were housed in a bunch of sheds surrounded by razor wire and several armed guards. His grandmother, my great-grandmother, came to see him every day, but they would never let them talk. The holding area was so small that my father could see his grandmother pleading with the guard at the front, crying and begging on her knees. He had no idea what was going to happen to them. They were interrogated every day, but he said nothing.

After about a week, a guard woke him early in the morning. He told my father to come with him. My father was brought to the front gate where there was a guard on duty that my father knew from school — the big quiet kid he always gave half his sandwich to. He opened the gate and motioned for my father to leave but did not speak.

My father went back to being a guerilla with a new group of men — shooting at the very same men who had just released him — right up until the end of the war. The fellows, his friends that were in the German holding camp with him, were never seen again.

My father was released from a camp in Italy at the end of the war. He then went to Germany for a couple of years. I asked him once why he would go to a place filled with people who, just months prior, had wanted to kill him. He said that the German people did not want to kill anyone, it was all Hitler. They were blind, or just didn't want to see — it was a very bad time in history. When he went to Germany after the war, he met beautiful and kind people. He realized that he'd been just as blinded by the war, but now in Germany, everyone was so happy. "It was magical," he said. There was no crime or fighting of any kind —he would meet up with women and go dancing.

I really liked that story. My father was a storyteller, a jokester, always trying to make you smile. He was a very nice man unless you made him angry — then, look out. I figured out early on that my father and mother should never have met. They were polar opposites, naturally different. I believe they were in love at some point but by the time I was around, there was true bitterness, maybe even hatred between them. I don't remember ever seeing them hug, embrace, walk hand-in-hand, or even kiss each other. Having said that, I don't remember any of my friends' parents showing affection either. Perhaps it was the generation. What did I know? I was just a kid.

I tell people I grew up in East Vancouver, but our house was on the Burnaby side of Boundary Road, the border between the two cities. We had a split-level 1940s bungalow with a view of East Van's industrial area. Every house on our block had at least a couple of kids in the house, all a few years older than me.

I started to get into trouble early. I failed grade two and had to repeat it. I was no dummy, but I missed a lot of school and I *did* have a bit of a learning disability. In hindsight who the hell didn't have one in those days? Sure, now we talk widely about Attention Deficit Hyperactivity Disorder and Fetal Alcohol Syndrome, but back then I'm sure I was on both spectrums and they would plague me throughout my schooling. In that era, the kids who didn't have issues skyrocketed to the top, and the rest of us hid in class and hoped to pass.

I went to summer school in between grades two and three. My father was so disappointed that I had failed. The administration said if I completed summer school and the teacher recommended me for grade three, they would let me attend. At the end of the summer term, the teacher told me I had a learning disability and suggested I take grade three with assistance from the learning center. I had issues with concentration — sit me by a window and I wouldn't retain a thing from what was being taught. My mind was always working a hundred miles-per-hour, but rarely on anything school related. I was lazy and had no desire to apply myself — I hated school, just hated it. I started fighting in grade two, this little skinny kid with fists flying. The teacher didn't like me. I was that guy—the little shit that was always late and then disruptive in class.

When the teacher let my father know what I'd been up to at school, he was furious — again, you didn't want to be around him when he was mad. He would pull his belt out and hold it up as if to strike me. I would immediately stop whatever I was doing that angered him. He never actually hit me with that belt, but I remember him making that gesture hundreds of times. My father could look very mean, he had a nasty scar that ran from his nostril up his cheek towards his eye. I asked him about it once and he told me he got kicked by a horse when he was young; but the way he turned away after I asked made it clear he didn't want to talk about it.

While my father never hit me that I remember, my mother was an entirely different story. My sister and brother physically *fought* with my mom, only because she'd be drunk and come at them. And when she started coming at me, when I was old enough and into grade six, I fought her also. It seemed I always had two mothers: the amazing one I loved with all my heart, and the drunken evil one I despised. I never, at any point, actually hated my mother — but I blamed her for many things. Upon reflection, she was the easiest target to blame. For me, fighting became a weekly event. I would get challenged by kids to fight. Once you fought someone, another kid would hear about it and think they could take you. Wanting to look tough, they came after you, and on and on it went. Back then, I looked like a stick-person: skinny, white, and sickly. But for some reason, I seriously enjoyed the fighting. I rarely won, and almost every fight was in front of a couple dozen chanting kids. Now that I think back, I may have even liked losing — not sure why I say that, but I was certainly fine with it at the time.

On Saturdays and Sundays, I would walk through the neighbourhood with two or three of my buddies, and pass a group of kids from another school. Rarely would we walk by without a challenge. We responded, "You want to fight?" They would say, "One against one," and we would brawl. I learned early that there were two kinds of kids: some who really wanted to hurt you, others who just wanted to fight. I didn't get hurt very often and I rarely hurt a kid that was vulnerable.

I did hurt a kid once because he'd been teasing me for weeks. I tried to ignore him, but I actually thought he would kill me. Finally, he was chirping at me and I snapped and turned around, ran at him and took him to the ground. I started beating him and when I got on top of him, I kept punching him in the face until he started crying. Then I stopped. I didn't get off and there was a group of kids saying let him go, get off of him. I gave him one more right on the nose. It exploded with blood, and he started screaming. He'd been bugging me for weeks, but I'm not sure why I did that — it came out of nowhere — and for the first time, I felt bad about hitting a kid that hard. He never bothered me again.

My elementary school was broken into two separate buildings. One was for grades four to seven, and the other was kindergarten to grade three, with the gym separating the spaces. Even though we were all on the same property, students were told to stay on their respective sides. We would be questioned if caught on the older school side while in grade three. That year I started being an 'anti-authority' type of kid. I would regularly go over to the older side and walk around there to see if any teachers would challenge me. No one ever did or even seemed to care.

Every so often there were exciting emergency response incidents like a fire, a shooting, or a suicide. Shots were fired at our neighbour's home across the lane, and a nice German woman was killed. One time a sniper set up a few blocks away on Georgia St, killing three people during a twelve-hour stand-off, ending when the sniper was shot and killed by police. I remember the morning after, riding over on my banana-seat bike and seeing all the police cars in front, then going into the back and riding down the lane. They had pulled all the carpet and underlay out into the backyard and it was covered in blood. I remember thinking that was so cool, and I would tell my friends about it. I wanted to be cool and looked for anything that would make it so — right then, that story was it.

The neighbourhood was made up of mostly Italians with the odd Chinese and Dutch family in the mix. No one really knew their neighbours more than a block away. Everyone kept to themselves outside of their immediate property line. So, when there was a shooting or a suicide, it didn't really change what you were going to have for dinner. In fact, I think it just became a part of life in the neighbourhood. I spoke to one of the kids who lived across the street from the sniper incident and he said the emergency response team was actually *in* his house. The whole family was hiding under the kitchen table for over eight hours. I was so jealous. He had this amazing adventure to tell and I didn't. I only had my story of riding up and seeing all the blood on the carpet, and that was not as good. In my neighbourhood, the important thing was the 'cool' story you could tell other kids to impress them.

I really liked the German lady across the street, and it made me sad that she was dead, but you don't quite understand the real meaning of death when you're seven years old. A few years later, my other neighbour (who lived next door to the German lady) hanged himself. That affected me. I really liked him. With an abundance of tools in his garage, he was always so willing to help me if I needed something fixed. He hanged himself in that same garage. That was the first time I really tried to understand death. But I wondered a lot more about the actual process of getting the rope ready and then stepping up to do it, rather than wondering *why* he did it. That was the first time in my life I really thought about suicide and the process of someone taking their own life, and death, in their hands.

We had no rules when we were kids especially after our parents went to bed. Mine usually got loaded, and I'm pretty sure they forgot they even had kids. In the summer, we started doing really stupid stuff, like messing around on Williams Street. It was one of the steepest streets in the neighbourhood and it ran through two busy roads: Boundary Road and Douglas Street. We used to get tires from the industrial area, sometimes from semi-trucks, that still had the rims, and we'd roll them down Williams Street and run like hell, listening to loud bangs and screeching as these tires went flying through the intersection. Some t-boned cars and totally crushed in the sides of the doors and fenders. It makes me cringe now when I think of how stupid we were as kids.

I remember my buddy Rich sawing on this massive tree in the bushes on Douglas Street. Now, this wasn't some little side street — this is a major street coming off Boundary Road, entering Burnaby. After hours of work, over a couple days, the tree came crashing down across the street in the middle of rush hour traffic, closing the road for hours. We thought that was so awesome, so hilarious!

One day, that same summer, the police came to our house asking if I had been breaking windows at the school. I had, but it was months ago, and they were talking about something that had happened that day. Funny thing is, I wasn't involved, but my dad was standing there so I admitted doing it, even though I wasn't there. My dad pulled out his belt and held it up. I remember being down on the ground, curled up in a ball, with him threatening me, but never hitting me. He should have, you know. It might have smartened me up a lot sooner on the long road to becoming a better kid.

CHAPTER FOUR

Cry Baby

Every kid in Vancouver dreaded the last weekend of the Pacific National Exhibition (PNE) because it meant another school year start was just around the corner. I grew up a few blocks away from the site of the biggest fair and amusement park in the province and over the years, my friends and I concocted several ways of getting into the PNE without paying. My friends liked making up counterfeit tickets, but I just liked climbing over the barbed wire fence. I'm not sure who actually thought that fence would keep anyone out. All you needed was a cut bleach bottle and a piece of cardboard to lay down, and then you were over.

One day, walking home from the PNE, my buddies and I came across another group of kids. We started eye balling each other. I was the skinny kid in our group, and there was a younger kid in the other group so we paired off and started fighting. The kid absolutely destroyed me. He had me down on the ground before I knew what was happening and hit me three or four times in the head. They all laughed and then left our group alone. We didn't talk much as we walked back to our part of the neighbourhood. I didn't feel bad about getting beat. I had never seen that group of kids before, so what did I care? My buddies, however, seemed humiliated.

This was a big year because I was moving from the small side of the school to the big side of elementary school, grades four to seven. It was kind of ominous, the kids in grade seven were known monsters, so I just tried to keep my head down that year. I got into a fight during recess only three months in, then a couple more just before Christmas.

Around that time, I started playing road hockey out on the corner near my house. I played almost every other night until 10:00 pm, just me and a tennis ball. It was the best way to get out of the house when my parents were fighting. I could still hear them, but I was focusing on scoring the winning goal in the Stanley Cup, over and over, to block out the yelling and screaming coming from my house a few hundred yards away.

Amidst the usual chaos in my home, there was one constant — spaghetti dinner on Saturday night at five o'clock and the voices of Dick Irvin and Danny Gallivan on Hockey Night in Canada. I loved those nights, with the smell of the food cooking, the show's theme song, and the start of the game.

Friday and Saturday were big drinking nights in my household which meant the biggest fights of the week. My mom would go at my sister or father and something would get broken, or someone would grab a knife and threaten someone else, and the police would get called. Mom always went for the knives. My brother did once, but I never saw my sister do it. I did it myself a couple times that year, threatening to kill myself in front of my mom. It had no effect. She fell on the floor crying, saying "Why?" repeatedly and stole the attention I was trying to get. Somehow it always turned into her moment. That was her line: "*Why?*" I never really understood what *why* meant. Now I think it meant something like: *Why was I born? Why is this happening to me? Why did I end up with such a loser family?* She got drunk very quickly when she came home from work. Her words were so slurred that she was hard to understand. When she would get really drunk, my Dad would carry her to bed once she passed out. Then he would go back to his La-Z-Boy easy chair and drink his beer, never looking at me if I was sitting in the room with him. He seemed like such a focused man, so much going on inside that head, but that stoic look and the movement bringing his chipped beer mug to his mouth was a robotic routine.

Looking back, I was starting to see why, to my parent's way of thinking, life was so cruel to them. I believe they should never have met. They hated their jobs, and being stuck in their crappy house, in a crappy little neighbourhood.

The police came a lot that year. Many times, I was out shooting the ball on the corner when they pulled up and walked into my house. In the run-down of the fights, my brother always came to the defense of my mom and threatened my dad. Greg accused my father of never treating him well. He would retell the story of how he found out my dad was not his real father; how, when he found my mom and dad's wedding picture, he saw himself, as a child, in the photo. He was always hostile to my dad after that.

On the other hand, I have memories of my childhood that make me smile. We made the most of what we had as kids. Aside from learning to become little criminals, we were always trying to show off to each other. We set up jumps and flew over them with our bikes. There were no shocks, no padding, just junky old banana-seat bikes which made for hard landings. We used to put down a couple of garbage cans under the ramps and jump them, only one or two, and then one of my buddies tried three, and couldn't do it. I was at school when I heard someone crashed trying for three cans so, naturally, I said I could jump five cans. Of course, I knew I couldn't, and the guy who tried three cans was a way better bike rider than me. I would crash on three too, so why the hell not say that I could do five? I was going to crash and burn anyway.

After school that day, a handful of kids found, or rather stole, five garbage cans from various neighbours' garages and set up the ramp. I went way up the lane and came screaming down, knowing full well I was going to crash. I got way up in the air and came down sideways on the fourth garbage can, everybody laughing at me. I hit the ground hard. My forks broke off, and the wheel went rolling away down the lane. Everyone was laughing, but I wasn't hurt and, aside from my busted bike, I was pretty proud of myself. I cleared the third and squashed the fourth and fifth one. They still laughed and one kid called me a loser, but I left them with the impression I had balls. And now that I think back, that was definitely what I was trying to accomplish. When you're a skinny little kid hanging out with 'cool' boys a couple of years older, you are always trying to prove yourself and show off. I heard one of them talking about how crazy I was days later. That really made me feel good, like I was fitting in.

As it turns out, grade four in the big school was anticlimactic. I ended up keeping my head down for the most part and got through without much drama. One of the coolest things about that year was my mom giving me a dollar to buy lunch at the White Spot restaurant every day, which was only a few blocks from my school. Every school day, Mom made me toast and jam as usual before she went to work and left a dollar beside the plate. I walked the three blocks from school and ordered the famous Pirate Pack—a hamburger, fries, pop, ice cream and a wrapped chocolate — all for one dollar. In the early 1970s, there was intense competition between restaurants like White Spot and McDonald's to gain low-income customers by claiming they could provide a meal for a single dollar.

At home, once a week, I was forced to eat the liver and onions my mother would cook. I would smother it with ketchup to hide the sour taste of the liver. It always triggered my gag reflex. But most nights of the week, I ate Swanson TV dinners, unless my dad made his special canned spaghetti sauce with parmesan cheese. Swanson TV dinners were about a buck-fifty each and they were *so good*. You could get a 'Turkey Dinner,' or 'Fish and Chips,' or my favourite, 'Salisbury Steak' with mashed potatoes and apple pie. We even had these cool TV dinner stands made of aluminum that weighed about a pound and folded up after you used them. It was a rare Saturday night, if no one was fighting, and if I had spaghetti or a TV dinner and a Pepsi watching Hockey Night in Canada. It was pure heaven.

Summer came, which was always a happy time. I passed grade four with very low grades and a big notation on my report card that said, "This student was part of LAC," (learning assistance class) and *that* did not make my father proud. But he loved me. I was his little boy. I think he even enjoyed that I got into fights and was pleased I was now playing baseball and soccer. What he didn't like was that I wasn't book smart. Both my brother and sister were straight-A students, and then there was me, in a special education class. Oh well, it was summer, and I didn't have to worry about that. I loved the holidays.

One day, two of my buddies and I were walking to our elementary school. My one friend turned to me and asked if I could break into the gym. I said no because it had panic bars, but I *could* get into the school through another door and enter the gym from the inside. The school had a monitored alarm so, if we got in, we only had about ten minutes to do whatever we were going to do. I finessed the secondary entrance door by sliding a piece of metal next to the doorknob plunger and then pushing and pulling until the door opened. We were in.

We opened all three of the gym recreation rooms then kicked and threw about three-hundred balls all over the gym. Suddenly, a car pulled up.

I peeked outside and, sure enough, it was the RCMP.

"Let's go out the door on the other side", I whispered. I looked back as we walked out —you couldn't even see the floor in the gym because of all the balls. It was awesome. When we get outside and up the street a bit, we saw several police cars responding with their lights shining on the school.

"Don't they have anything better to do?" my buddy joked, and we all laughed.

Now we are three stupid elementary kids walking up the street when a police car came flying, driving right onto the sidewalk to block us from running. The cop gets out and he is furious. He slams his hand on the front of his police car and asks, "Did you shit-rats just break into the school?" I respond by asking what school he was talking about, and he smashed his hand down again. "Don't get fucking smart with me, I will throw you in this car right now and wipe that fucking shit-eating grin right off your face." I shut up. He was intimidating. My buddy blurted out, "We weren't anywhere near the school!" And the officer replied that he had an eyewitness saying three kids just left the side door of the gym. I was terrified now, but I wasn't going to say a damn thing. My buddy said, "Honest officer, it wasn't us, we weren't at the school." The cop stared at my buddy. I just looked at the ground.

He got back into his car without saying anything and drove away. We ran to a friend's house nearby and laid low in his yard until we thought the cops had left the neighbourhood. This was the first time in a long time that I had been confronted by the police. My heart had felt like it was going to explode out of my chest as I was talking to him. I was impressed with myself for keeping my cool.

I've broken into a lot of things — buildings, cars, trucks— but never anyone's house. Like the officer said, I was a shit-rat of a kid for sure; I stole people's Christmas lights, raided their gardens, stuck potatoes in car exhaust pipes, shoplifted stuff from stores, broke into schools and commercial buildings. But I never broke into a house.

My best buddy Rich and I used to hang out in the back lane, where we would meet the rest of the neighbourhood kids. When Fridays came around and it got dark, we gathered to decide what we were going to do that night.

Nicky-nicky-nine-doors, breaking and entering, blowing something up — it all depended on who was in the lane that night.

One day Rich and I were hanging out. We saw Ruutu coming down the lane with a couple of other neighbourhood guys. He said he had something to show us. Ruutu was from one of the three Finnish families down the block. They were kind of strange, at least to us kids at the time. They ate dried fish and week-old boiled eggs, had amazing tans and great skin, and they all looked ten years younger than they were. There was one guy, a single Finn that lived in a big house all by himself, with no wife, no kids. He was a legend. We called him 'Juicy,' but I never knew why. He drove a Saab. I had never seen a car like it. He was always super friendly and nice to us, asking all the kids how they were doing. We thought he was cool.

Meeting up in the lane, Ruutu said that he was house-sitting for Juicy and that we should all come over. Something didn't seem right, but I didn't care, I couldn't help but want to see the inside of Juicy's place. So, I and four other grade four and five kids ended up going to Juicy's house. Ruutu brought us up to the front door and told us to wait. I thought it was strange that he needed to walk around the back of the house if he was house-sitting. Within minutes he opened the front door and invited us in. I didn't realize it then, but this was the first time that we kids were actually breaking into a home. Ruutu took us to a back room in the basement and told us to sit on the floor. There were no windows in this room, just a Super 8mm projector and a screen. Ruutu seemed to know everything about the room, as if he had been there several times before. I found out later that Juicy had gone back to Finland for a month. Ruutu knew this and had found an open window and had been going in and out of the house for a couple of weeks.

So, there we were, a handful of eleven-year-olds watching Ruutu as he got a chair, stood on it, and moved a part of the suspended ceiling to grab three movie reels. No one spoke a word, all of us wondering what the hell was on those movie reels, and how the hell Ruutu knew they were in some secret part of the ceiling. He fed the movie reel through the projector as if he worked at a cinema. We were his stunned audience. The projector warmed up, and I remember the moment as if it were yesterday, a room of young kids totally silent for an entire minute, like it was the greatest release of a motion picture ever.

The projector finally signaled it was ready, and Ruutu started the film. It was some strange home movie. The first scene was Juicy cooking in his kitchen, just upstairs in the house we were in, with a Finnish-looking woman who I'd never seen before. They were drinking wine and the camera must have been on the counter for the first scene but then moved around the room so the scenes would stop and start a lot. They started kissing and fondling each other, and then they were on the couch, removing their clothes. I'm pretty sure I went into shock right then and there. We were a group of kids watching a random guy that we knew from our neighbourhood taking some woman's clothes off. It was mesmerizing. Then they started to have sex, right there in his kitchen. I had never seen a sexual act before, and while I had no idea what was happening, the guys I was with certainly seemed to understand. I kept wanting to ask what was happening. We continued to watch in silence and, after what seemed hours, Juicy pulled his penis out and came. I yelled, "What the hell is that?" referring to the ejaculation part. Everyone looked at me, and one of my buddies started laughing as if I was joking. We sat for some time, watching several of his movies where he was with women on his balcony, the same balcony we kids walked by all the time, and he was out there screwing them in broad daylight.

When I left Juicy's home, so many things were racing through my mind. This was my first introduction to sex, and it really impressed me. Now, I knew Ruutu was *not* house sitting, and was pretty sure we were in that house illegally. But I still had no idea what came out of Juicy's penis! I wasn't experiencing puberty yet, and we only had three black-and-white TV channels and a radio, so my ability to search for answers was limited. One day, I asked one of the kids who had been there about it but didn't get much of an answer. The other thing that I could never get out of my mind was, how did Ruutu know what was in that room? He took those movies out of the ceiling as if he knew they were there. Did Juicy show them to him? And why the hell was his name "Juicy?" No one ever told me that. I never asked Ruutu how he knew. It would be kept as a secret forever — Ruutu committed suicide several years later.

That summer went by so fast. before I knew it, it was the start of grade five. I was always anxious about the first day of school because I never knew who my teacher was until I walked up and looked at the list on the door. I was in Mr. Clarke's class, the strictest teacher in the big school. No one had ever seen him laugh and he hated troublemakers. I was lucky because for that first term, I spent half the day in LAC (learning assistance), and the rest in Mr. Clarke's class.

September and October flew by. I liked the way Mr. Clarke taught. He was intimidating, but he wrote kind notes on my work. For the first time ever, I had a teacher who was trying to inspire me. I don't think he liked me much, but every kid in the class could say the same thing. He never smiled, just did what he had to do and dealt with things effectively. Once, I put some tacks on a kid's seat, and he screamed out in class. Mr. Clarke said, "Who did this?" I put up my hand. He walked over to me, grabbed me by the ear, dragged me out of class and walked me right down to the principal's office. He said, "If you ever do anything else like that in my class again, you will seriously regret it." He asked me if I understood — and I did. It was the first time I had ever been disciplined like that.

November flew past without any issues, as I did not want to be punished again by Mr. Clarke. He terrified me and for once, I even came to class on time. He had a good grasp on dealing with kids — fair but very firm.

Christmas was around the corner, and my mom and dad were happy with me for not getting into trouble at school. They promised me I would get the minibike I had been drooling over for the last year-and-a-half, because I had "turned the corner" as my father said. Greg said he had made a lot of money at the fish cannery that year and was going to get me a super cool race car set. He gave me a picture of the set, and I posted it on my wall along with a ripped-out page of the Sears catalogue of the minibike. I looked at it every night before I went to bed.

Aside from a few fights, I had been really good that year and was so excited as Christmas neared. The build-up to that Christmas morning was the biggest I ever remember. Greg, who was then twenty-two, and I always talked about the race car set. It was one of those double lane electric track ones with *three freaking loops* — the biggest set at the Hudson's Bay store. I dreamed about riding my minibike during the day and playing with the race car set at night. I was struggling to get to sleep because I was so excited.

On my way home from school one day, I saw a big Sears truck a couple of blocks away, close to my house. *Oh my god*, I thought, *it's trying to drop off the minibike*. But no one was home! I could see the truck starting to move, so I started running. I was in a full sprint as it turned the corner and proceeded down the street. I kept following the truck, but it made a left and headed up to Boundary Road, so I gave up and went home. I was sure they would try again after their next stop. That night, I waited at the window for hours, but the Sears truck never showed. Maybe they only delivered once a day, I thought.

I told my mom that they may have tried to deliver that day and she should call them to tell them that delivering it tomorrow, after three-thirty, would be best. But she was drinking already, gave me a "yeah, yeah" motion with her hand, and took another drag on her cigarette. My mother was a heavy-duty smoker. She went through packs and packs a day. If she passed out at the kitchen table, her cigarette would roll out of her fingers onto the table or the floor. Our furniture, floors and a few curtains had burn marks all over them. When I think about all the calls I've responded to as a firefighter and how many of them are caused by smoking, it's a miracle our house didn't burn down.

School in grade five was going well, but I spent half the day in LAC and the other kids used to bug me about "being a dummy." There was this one chubby older kid who used to taunt me: "Going to the special class today? Do they give you drugs in there to try and make you smarter? Do they?" And all the kids would laugh, but I ignored him. It bothered me that the other kids were laughing, but not what he was saying.

By then, I had accepted I wasn't smart. The teacher said there was something wrong, that my brain had not made all the right connections. With time, she said, I would be able to figure stuff out with the tools I was learning to use. She was the nicest teacher with an amazing smile, and she seemed to understand me. This was one of the few times in my life I actually took notice of how things were getting better, like school, and not fighting as much, plus I was about to get the two greatest gifts a boy could ever receive. So yeah, life was good at that point.

The day before Christmas Eve, I was so excited about my gifts, but also a little anxious because I couldn't remember a single Christmas Eve where everyone didn't get loaded and start fighting. I had searched everywhere in my home, but I couldn't find where they were hiding the minibike. I started to think they must have stored it at someone else's house because it was so big.

I woke up early that morning. On a weekend, waking up was usually noon or one in the afternoon for me. My brother wouldn't get up until three. We were brutally lazy kids. Most of our weekends would pass like that—we slept it away.

Mom was at the grocery store, getting the last little tidbits for turkey dinner, and Dad was watching sports on TV. Tomorrow would be one of the only days we all sat at a table as a family. But then the drinking would start, and the fighting, and the whole thing would be short-lived.

Uncle Danny always came over for Christmas Eve. If he was still alive today, he could tell some great family stories I'm sure. He never married, and we were his only real connection to a semblance of family life. When I think about it now, it's no wonder he never got married.

By five o'clock on that Christmas Eve, my mom was already drunk, firing out insults at whoever was in earshot. She and my brother went at it first, and then my dad yelled, "Goddammit, can't we have *one* Christmas where people aren't fighting?" Somehow, my brother took that to mean my father didn't love him because my mother had him with another man. Greg went on a rant, telling my dad about all the things he had never done for him, all the stuff he had never bought for him, and how he was a brutal father. Before I knew it, my mother was pulling up her pant legs to show off her varicose veins, screaming at my father. They attacked him relentlessly as he sat in the La-Z-Boy with a beer in his hand, just staring out the window.

After what seemed like hours, I went to my room, crawled into bed and cried. That's what I did all the time — hid in my bed and covered my ears. I could usually fall asleep through the fighting but not that night. It was Christmas Eve. Finally, I couldn't stand them attacking my dad any longer. I loved the guy. I got out of bed and ran into the kitchen yelling at everyone to shut up, it was Christmas and the neighbours could hear us! I saw my father's eyes well up.

Greg didn't stop, he didn't care, and just went on shouting at my dad. My mother looked at me and called me pathetic. She said I was a pain in the ass, their biggest disappointment as parents, and that she was ashamed of me. I had heard all of that before, so it wasn't too painful, but what she said next put me into shock. Mom was trying to get up and walk towards me, but was too drunk, so she just stood there swaying, and blurted out: "And that minibike you wanted, well we never even ordered it, you spoiled little brat!"

I was stunned. I looked at my dad. He had his head in his hands now and was fully crying. I asked, "Dad, that's not true is it?" And when he didn't lift his head, I knew it was true.

I ran at my mother and shoved her, sent her flying to the floor. She started crying. My brother swore at us all and retreated to his room in the basement. Mom was on the floor yelling that I'd broken her back, and my dad still had his head in his hands.

I retreated to my room and cried. When I stopped, I put on my clothes and went outside. I walked down to the foundry in the rain and broke into the building. At 11 years old, I had developed a knack for lock breaking. I'm not sure why I was good at it, but doors and simple locks were easy to jimmy. The foundry mainly made car parts and aside from a few hanging light bulbs, it was a huge empty building with a dirt floor and several big melting crucibles. It had a tin roof that was partly open where the rain poured in and ran across the floor into a drain. It was spooky, but I felt safe there by myself. It was just above freezing, and I was soaked from the walk, but I sat on a welder's bench and cried.

After a couple hours, I decided to go home to bed. When I was close, I could see three police cars outside my house. I could hear my brother screaming, "I am going to sue! You'll get fired!" The cops had him cuffed and were bringing him down the stairs. I went inside and my mother was yelling at the officers. By the look on their faces, I could see they were thinking we were rats. A loser family. One of the officers was talking to my dad, but I just walked past and went to my room. I had seen this dog-and-pony show before, and this Christmas was standard. I went into my room and threw my wet clothes on the ground, crawled into the lower part of my bunk bed, and stared at the ceiling until I fell asleep.

The next morning, I woke up to Christmas day without my usual excitement. I dragged my butt out of bed and went out to the tree. There were lots of presents underneath, but no big box that could have held the race car set. Nothing had been opened.

My sister was up, my dad was having a coffee, and my mom was around somewhere. I went to my stocking. It was filled with a couple of mandarin oranges and some candies. That was my mom's big thing, putting oranges in the stockings. I liked it, though I always wanted more toys. To be honest, I can't recall what I got that year, but I know it wasn't a race car set or a minibike.

This was the first time I remember feeling depressed. I felt like I had no energy. I couldn't muster the feeling to do anything. When Greg came home from the police lock-up, he didn't speak to anyone in the house for weeks. He was furious with my father for not sticking up for him before the police took him away. I asked him about the race car set, and he said he was just a little tight for cash that Christmas. For sure, he would get me one next year.

In the end, he never did buy one for me, and I never asked him about it again. I was so excited thinking I was going to get that race car set, but all along, I should have known better.

CHAPTER FIVE

Train Wreck

Weeks went by and I was still feeling sorry for myself. I had little interest in being social. In fact, I wasn't motivated to do much of anything. Like a heavy anchor dragging behind me, my home life never changed, and it never would.

Another typical weekend came along, filled with lots of drinking. My mother and father were having a classic battle, so I just went to my room. After about an hour of crashing, smashing, and yelling, I stormed out of my room and shouted that I hated them both. I remember thinking that seriously, I wanted them to just die. I know that sounds awful, but I was exhausted and hated my family life so much — there seemed no hope for a better future.

For me to say that, I guess I really did hate them at that moment. I loved them too because they were such great people when sober, but I'd finally given up on them. I didn't understand the power of addiction. My parents were clinically depressed, but no one talked about that in those days. It's woefully apparent now. Instead of medication, they drank it away.

Anyway, I was done — just done, and started to cry when I was yelling at them. My mother was loaded, but I remember the way she laughed at me, a real belly laugh. She was mocking me, and I think it was the first time I really wanted to kill someone.

So I packed my backpack with a couple pairs of socks, underwear, blue jeans, and a sweatshirt. I opened the envelope in my desk and took out all eighty-two dollars and fifty-six cents. I was leaving.

I didn't have a great plan, but I figured I would go down Lougheed Highway at Gilmour Street to where there was a bend in the railway tracks. I would just get on the next big train and see where it took me. That area had a creek running through it where we used to poke rats and catch crayfish. I had seen the train slow down on the corner many times as we searched the creek bed for critters and things. I had never jumped on a moving train before, but I wondered how hard it could be. I had seen people do it in the movies all the time.

As I left, I saw Dad in his La-Z-Boy with a beer and a blank stare. The fighting had settled for now, but it never really stopped. My mom would get tired and then start up again. Why the hell was my dad still living with her? He was so unhappy. Walking through the kitchen, Mom — or rather, the evil version of Mom — looked up at me and scowled in a slurred voice, "Where are you going?" I took a last look at her and felt bad, not sure when I might see her again. I hoped she would be okay because I still really loved her.

It was about nine-thirty on a Tuesday night, and I was happy about one thing: there would be no school for tomorrow — I would be on a train to happiness. This makes it sound like I was a really strong kid — I wasn't. I cried like a baby as I walked to the tracks. It was pouring rain and my shirt was already soaked through to my skin. It took me thirty minutes to get to the train tracks. I was entirely soaked, and clearly had not thought this one through. I would be out of dry clothes if I changed now. So I sat there for two hours. No train came. There was no place to get out of the rain, and I was freezing cold. Another hour went by with no train.

Four and a half hours later, well after midnight, I could hear the train off in the distance. I leapt to my feet. I was ready to change my life and this train, wherever it was going, was taking me to a fantastic place. As the train straightened out along the line, its light shone straight into my eyes, blinding me. It was insanely bright. I couldn't see anything but that blazing white light. It stunned me. I could feel the vibration as the train rumbled closer. Then it was upon me. As soon as the engine went by, I could see again.

Oh my god, the train was huge, like three storeys high, going stupidly fast. My mind began to race, and I started to run beside the train. It was still going way faster than me. I looked for a ladder or something to grab, but there was nothing. As it rolled by me, I suddenly became terrified. It was so big, it was the loudest thing I had ever heard, and it was going faster than ever now that I was up close.

I remember thinking I had seen this train hundreds of times when I was down in the creek whacking rats with a stick or catching crayfish. This was the same train that went by all the time with a couple of engines, boxcars, and a caboose. Now that I was up close, it was a very different beast.

The rocks along the train tracks were huge, sharp boulders. They were difficult to walk on even without the rain, and impossible to run on now, as I scrambled for the caboose. I couldn't even attempt to grab the handrail. It was too high and the beast was going way too fast! Before I knew it, the caboose flew by me. Just like that, the chance to change my life was gone.

I didn't make the train.

Now I was soaking wet, frozen to the bone and didn't have any food. I had missed my ticket to paradise. By then, I was sure my parents must have realized I'd run away and would call the police to search for me. But maybe, I thought, when they punch my name into the computer and see who it is, they might not be in much of a hurry to find me. I was a pain in the ass not only to my parents, but to my neighbours, teachers, and especially the police.

My elementary school had this crawl space under the gym that I used to hang out in — I figured this should be my next move. I walked to the school and hunkered down until I could figure out what to do next.

I wasn't going home, that was for sure. I was wet, shivering, and hungry, but I had money. I could take a bus somewhere, maybe up North. My aunt and uncle lived in Yellowknife in the Northwest Territories, maybe I could head up there and see how things went along the way. Different options raced through my mind as I curled up in the corner, but I was so damn cold. I started to hear noises and see shadows moving around in the distance. Fear started to come over me as I sat there. Suddenly, there was a loud noise and I jumped to my feet. I ran outside and looked around, but it was too dark to see anything.

I decided to get on the move again, walking towards Hastings Street, the main road to downtown Vancouver. It was about three-thirty in the morning, and there were no cars on the streets. Rainwater squished out of my runners as I walked. I didn't feel as afraid when I was under the streetlights of Hastings.

I sat down at a bus stop, and an overwhelming feeling came over me. I started to cry again. After thirty minutes or so, I seriously thought about what I was doing. I had no plan. I was starving, soaking wet, and had eighty bucks in my pocket — what the hell could I do? At the end of another half hour, I gave in. I would go home and figure out a plan for another day. I was sure my parents would be awake and looking for me. My father would be furious, and I would actually get the belt this time, but I didn't care. I hated my life already, so getting beaten wouldn't be the worst thing in the world. The police would have to be notified that I had returned home, and I was sure there would be some follow up by social services. The escape hadn't gone exactly how I'd wanted but at least I had caught everyone's attention.

As I walked up to my house, I could see the kitchen light was on. I was sure someone would be in there pacing the room waiting for me. Maybe it would be Mom, and she would hug me if she were sober. I was desperately hoping that was the case. I walked into the kitchen and was hit with the stench of nicotine from years of my mother's smoking. There was the clunky sound of our old fridge starting up — but no one was there. *Maybe they are out looking for me,* I thought. For the first time, I started to feel bad about what I had done. It had been childish, but I had been furious. I went through the house but there were no lights on in the hall and the bedroom doors were closed. I opened the door of my mom and dad's room. They were sound asleep in their bed. There was no search, no beating for me, and no social services intervention. They didn't care.

I flopped down on my bed, in my soaking wet clothes, and started to cry again. I cried all the time, and it got me nowhere. I hated myself, my life, and my family. Lying there in that bed, at eleven years old, I thought about different ways to kill myself.

I made it through the remainder of grade five without much drama but I was still an angry and depressed little kid, getting into the same old trouble like breaking windows at the school or down in the industrial area, jimmying building door locks open to see what was inside.

We did our usual stuff that summer, rolling tires down Williams Street so they would hit moving cars coming through the intersection. We hung out at the bottom of Boundary Road and built a fort in the bushes. We made up a cool tree-bending game where we would climb as high as we could on the skinny alder trees in that area. Then, as high as we dared, we would start to sway back and forth until it bent over and broke. The idea was to grab onto the next tree before you fell, and repeat the swaying, bending, and breaking. Occasionally, you would come crashing down to the ground.

The other game we played was called "pass out." You would stand against a wall and take ten deep, fast breaths and then someone would push hard on your chest, and you would pass right out. It was weird because some of my buddies would be unconscious for about ten or fifteen seconds and would start thrashing around as if having seizures. In hindsight, I'm sure the game wasn't good for us, but we used to spring it on anyone who hadn't seen it done before — especially when they said there was no way it would work. We did it to this one kid at school and, when he passed out, my buddy stepped away. The kid fell like a tree and smashed his face into the ground. He was totally out cold, different from the others. Another kid ran and got the principal. When he asked what happened, we all looked at each other and said we didn't know, that he just passed out. That poor kid was away for weeks, apparently in the children's hospital for all kinds of testing with his parents freaking out. We were one stupid group of kids, so cocky — and so lucky that we didn't kill ourselves or someone else.

My parents were still fighting, with the police making multiple visits to my home that year. I played road hockey past midnight every night, even on school nights. Just me on the corner with a net, stick, and a tennis ball scoring the winning goal and hoisting the Stanley Cup. On Saturday night I watched hockey with my dad, but if my Mom wasn't working that weekend she would start drinking in the morning, and then the fighting would start mid-afternoon, and stop when either my mom passed out or the police came. I left on those nights, leaving my poor dad with her screaming at him, always the same argument: how he'd ruined her life, how she hated him. Then she would pull the classic pant leg trick, showing her calves and thighs and saying, "Look, look what you've done to me!"

Back then, I didn't understand why my father would not leave. But I get it now. They were dysfunctional as hell, but he really loved her. Maybe my mom felt the same whenever she was sober, but I wasn't so sure. She could, and did, say the nastiest things to him. In that era, you didn't hear of many divorces. I remember watching the Brady Bunch and wishing I lived with them, only to hear years later that Barry Williams, who played the oldest son, was sleeping with Florence Henderson, the mom.

Funny, how we perceive our lives while we're kids. I fell into a routine that summer that seemed to set the course of my childhood going forward. Shooting the ball into the empty net helped block out the madness of my family, even though I could hear them screaming as I took shot after shot.

One of the kid's dads from down the way was a firefighter — I used to think he was so cool. I was inspired and thought, *maybe I could be a firefighter?* That was the first time I saw a 'something' in my future. I would ride up to the fire hall closest to my house, the Number Five Fire Hall at Hastings and Willingdon. I'd sit there hoping to see them ride out on a call, but they didn't. I had no idea what schooling was needed to become a firefighter but thinking about more school discouraged me. I got on my bike and rode away.

I stopped talking to my parents, barely speaking to them over the few summer months. I'm fairly sure my dad was getting worried by the time grade six started. As usual, during the school term, Mom left me a plate of toast and jam every morning and a dollar to go to the White Spot and buy a Pirate Pack for lunch.

I was the only kid in school that walked down every day to the White Spot restaurant and bought a hamburger. It was an escape from school for an hour. I hated school. I was a skinny, ratty-looking kid, with a Sears jean jacket that I wore every day of my childhood until it was too small. In short, I was recognizable. Every day, the cooks had my hamburger ready on a plate when I walked in.

One evening, Dad said he was worried about me, and asked if I was okay. I told him I was fine. But it was obvious I wasn't happy. It was not in his vocabulary to say things like, "I love you," but I knew he did. He could see I was depressed.

Several things my dad chose to do that year positively affected me. It was as if a light switch flipped on for him. He decided I should play an instrument, any kind I wanted, so I started playing the drums. He put me in music lessons every Wednesday — an hour of learning to play and read music. The lessons were boring, but I had drums and played them every day.

We started skiing together on Sundays. Soon enough, he said I should join the ski team. I agreed. Ski racing sounded super cool, like jumping garbage cans with your bike, but better because you could win a genuine trophy.

Then Dad bought tickets to see the Vancouver Canucks. They were offering a half-season package at seven bucks and seventy-five cents per ticket that got us seats three rows from the top of the arena. My dad and I started going to Canucks games together and I loved it. Every game Dad would buy me a glass of Coke and a huge bag of chips. I would drink out of the bottle while he poured booze into a cup from a flask. Watching hockey live like that was a fantasy come true. The only downside was my dad made us leave with two minutes left so we could beat the traffic leaving the rink. He didn't care how close the game was, we always left early. Now that I think back, my father would have four to five ounces of gin in his little flask. That would make him impaired by today's standards. Technically, he was driving us home drunk from those games every time. In those days, everyone drank and drove, so it didn't seem unusual. Luckily, we were never in an accident. My dad was a master at maneuvering his massive Pontiac Parisienne home.

With these new father-son experiences, my outlook became more optimistic. My relationship with my father was truly special — so important in any child's life and critical for a lost kid like me.

I became a Canucks fan that year, and even though they sucked and lost over half their games, I loved it. With my dad involved in my life, I didn't feel like such a freak and a loser. For once, several things were bringing me actual joy. My mother, however, was struggling, working tons of overtime, and drinking more than usual. It was a tough year for her, but my defense was learning to ignore her as much as possible.

One day, the fire department brought a truck to my school for a fire prevention event. The firefighters looked cool in their uniforms, and the truck was magical — freshly cleaned and not a scratch to be found. They put the lights and siren on and, and just like that, I really wished I could be one of those guys. Yet the thought of more schooling to become a firefighter was like a bucket of cold water thrown over my head.

Although hockey was a big thing, by December I was ski racing on the Son of Norway Ski Team. After only one month of training, I had my first race. I placed third. It was the first time I had ever won a trophy. I had lots of ribbons from school sports days, but a trophy trumped all that.

A couple of other things happened that year, both involving cars.

Driving up Seymour Mountain one Sunday to a ski competition, there was a whiteout and we couldn't see a thing. A car suddenly appeared in front of us and we crashed into the back of it. It had been involved in an earlier accident and was at a standstill. If it wasn't totaled already, we finished it off. But unfortunately, our car was totaled also. Dad was crushed because he didn't have collision insurance. We were a paycheck-to-paycheck family.

In another incident, I watched my friend get run over by a car right in front of my eyes. I used to sit in my front window looking out and thinking about things. I could see the whole of the East Vancouver industrial area and the housing projects between Broadway and First Avenue. I was sitting and looking out one day, and a car came down the block. As it went through the intersection, my neighbour Ronnie, a kid a couple of years older than me, came flying out of a side street. Ronnie was in the middle of the road and was instantly crushed before the driver could react. The car drove right over him and stopped with Ronnie underneath screaming.

I paused, shocked. I was unsure of what had just happened. I could see the car stopped in the middle of the street, the male driver getting out and crouching down and looking under the car.

Then I was throwing on my runners and bolting out the front door. I was half a block away and could hear Ronnie screaming from under the car as I ran towards him. I screeched to a halt, turned around, and ran to Ronnie's house. His mother, Joan, was in the kitchen.

"Ronnie's been run over!" I screamed. She screamed back and we both ran to the intersection. The driver was yelling to call an ambulance when we arrived. One of the neighbours that had come out onto the street went back into her house and did so.

Ronnie's mom was hysterical. There was lots of blood under the car and I guess his arms and legs were pressed against the exhaust because you could smell flesh burning. At the time, all I could focus on was the screaming coming from under that car. Joan knew me well, but she wasn't fond of me and the trouble I caused in the neighbourhood. She was crying and yelling at me to grab towels from my house. I sprinted there and back, bringing a bundle of towels.

It felt like forever for the responders to get there. The firetruck came first and, in a flash, had the car jacked up. I was in awe watching. They were like superheroes, working perfectly in tandem, communicating back and forth. In less than a minute they had Ronnie removed from under the car. There were burns all over his body and face, his leg was clearly broken, and he was screaming even louder now. Watching Joan losing her mind over her son was surreal. Nevertheless, watching the procedure of Ronnie being loaded onto a gurney and taken away in the ambulance was cool.

When the crisis on the street calmed down, one of the firefighters asked if I wanted to come onto the truck. It blew my mind! They had these air-pack things for them to breathe in a fire, and all sorts of tools, it was like being on a spaceship. I'd forgotten all about Ronnie at this point and was totally and entirely consumed by thoughts of becoming a firefighter one day. Again, I blocked it out later because I could barely pass basic elementary school. But I wondered why I kept getting exposed to firefighters. It's killing me that I'll never be one, I thought.

As it turned out, Ronnie was okay. He fully recovered in just over a month. As far as I was concerned, it was the firefighters who saved his life.

Todd, Mike, Rich and I broke into the foundry one weekend. The break-in itself wasn't a big deal — we'd done that on several occasions, I even did it myself the night I tried to run away — but this time, Todd thought it would be a neat idea to take gas out of the cannisters stored over in the welding area. One of the bottles was labeled *Oxy Acetylene*. None of us had any idea what it was but thought we should pour it into a container and light it on fire. We found a box of big black garbage bags and held one over the nozzle, turning on the oxy acetylene until it filled up. We tied it off and brought it out to the interior parking lot surrounded by another three warehouses. It was impossible to see the area from the main street.

For the first time in all our hijinks, I didn't want any part of this. I wanted out of there, but I didn't go. I had this nagging feeling—it just felt wrong. Plus, no one had any matches. I didn't want to look like a chicken in front of my buddies, but I was looking for a way to leave, an easy out. When we realized that no one had matches we agreed to go to the corner store and get some. While we were inside, I managed to fake a look at the clock on the wall and say, "Holy shit, I have to go or my dad is going to kill me!" They didn't care, and I ran home.

They went back to the interior parking lot to light the bag on fire. I guess when they got there, they too were a little hesitant. They probably all had that same worried, nagging feeling I did, but they didn't act on it. Mike tried to keep his distance by flicking matches off the strip on the pack, shooting little missiles at the bag of gas.

On the fifth flick, the match hit the bag. It exploded! Mike was sent flying backward, the explosion strong enough to blow out all the windows in the surrounding warehouses for half a block. Todd was far enough away to remain on his feet, but Mike was thoroughly stunned and couldn't get his feet underneath him to run. It took them several minutes to screw their heads back on and start running. The alarms had gone off in the adjoining warehouses and they could hear the approaching sirens as they sprinted.

Three blocks away, I heard the explosion in my backyard. It wasn't a sharp sound but more of a deep bass, a kind of whomping sound. For once, I was afraid and worried that one of our adventures had gone seriously wrong. I think with the good things going on in my life, hearing a literal explosion I had participated in to some degree, suddenly woke me up. For once, I gave a shit. We all laid low after that misadventure.

It was June and grade six was almost over. The excitement of summer holidays was soon around the corner. I felt like I'd had a pretty good year and, for once, was not in any trouble at all. I was still in learning assistance and didn't mind school as much, even getting there on time some days. I got challenged to a fight in the park one night and, for the first time in my life, I turned it down. The guy walked beside me taunting. He was right up in my face calling me, "Chicken! Braaaauuuck brauk brauk! Come on chicken!" I had no idea why I didn't fight. Maybe I was afraid, maybe I'd been affected by that last brutal fight, I wasn't sure. I walked away, or chickened out, as the kid said.

On my final test in my learning assistance class, I received ninety percent. I was thrilled! I waited for Dad to come home to tell him. I could tell he was a little off when he got home; he cracked a beer and flopped into his easy chair without saying a word to me, but I thought this would cheer him up.

"Hey Dad, I got a test back today and I got ninety percent!"

He asked me if it was in that special class I was in. I knew where it was going immediately when he asked that, but I answered yes.

He said, without looking at me: "Congratulations. You're the smartest one in the dumb class."

I walked away, grabbed my hockey stick and shot the tennis ball until about 1:00 am that night, all those loser feelings flooding back.

I disappointed my father by not doing well in school, but I just couldn't get it. My brother and sister set the bar high, and in comparison, I was in freaking *learning assistance*. I guess my father had every right to be ashamed of me.

On that sour note, the summer started with little fanfare. My father was depressed, and my mother was in pitiful shape — something was going on, but I wasn't certain what it was.

That summer was different though. I stopped hanging out with Ruutu and some of the other kids. My other buddies were starting to experiment with drugs. There was a shop down on Main and Hastings that was selling this thing called "Rush." It was liquid that came in a little bottle that you held to your nostril and sniffed. It made you feel dizzy, like a head rush, and it became popular with school kids. Other kids were selling pot and suddenly everything was available. I recall feeling conflicted — I wanted to be cool, but the only way to be cool and accepted was sniffing rush or smoking pot. My buddies kept telling me it was relaxing and if I did it, I would stop thinking about my problems. I knew otherwise. Something I sniffed or smoked was not going to make my mom sober.

My common sense ruled. I didn't do any drugs that summer, none at all. I had my best friends, Rich and Paulo across the street, and although we were still getting into trouble with our parents for being such little shits, Paulo was from a strict Italian family and rarely got into the same amount of trouble as Rich and I. So I started hanging around with him more. He was a couple of years younger than me but hanging out with him was a positive direction to take.

I did some drinking while my friends sniffed rush and smoked pot. I got my first girlfriend, a girl named Sandra. It was all pretty innocent. She was a year younger than me and all we did was play spin the bottle. She and her friends were into smoking cigarettes, and I tried too, but aside from that, it was a tame summer.

When September rolled around, I was accepted into a split-classroom pilot of both grade sixes and sevens. We had no desks, just couches and communal workstations — I thought that was pretty cool.

I still had to attend learning assistance classes, but my teacher was Ms. Kelly. She was great at "inspiring" me. She was very attractive, and I was just hitting puberty. Many nights I would wake up and my bed was soaked from a wet dream. She was in most of them.

Puberty is a weird phase in a kid's life. Aside from watching Juicy's homemade porn tapes, the sexuality of becoming an adult was a total mystery to me. I didn't really understand what was happening, not in biological terms at least. I can't speak for all eleven-year-olds, but it was like a switch flipped in my brain — I turned from this little troublemaker to a horny kid obsessed with sex.

One day, a neighbour asked me to come over and help her get into her house. Her husband was out of town. She had locked herself out of the house, and she wanted me to climb in through her bedroom window and open the door. *Oh my god*, I'm thinking, *this is the moment. She's going to seduce me!* My neighbour was about forty years old — and my erotic thoughts got the best of me — I wet myself before I even got to the back door. Letting her in, she told me to follow her. In the kitchen, she said she had something for me. I stood there, completely wet, but it hadn't broken through my jeans. She gave me twenty-five cents — a freaking quarter! And then she thanked me again.

I kept imagining, over and over again, climbing through her window, opening the door, and making love to her in every room of that house. I was infatuated, thinking about her off and on for the next couple of years. She had massive boobs — well, young Steve thought they were massive — thinking back, they were probably an average size.

That was the start of puberty for me — wet dreams, erotic fantasies, every other night.

The first month of school flew by. The split-class was awesome, a good mix of younger and older, and I was falling in love with Ms. Kelly. She would lean over my shoulder when teaching me something, and I would just melt.

Hockey season started and Dad and I went to the games. Life was awesome, but far from perfect. My mom was still in a bad way — a real disaster. I had never seen her so constantly drunk. But the fighting and drinking at home was hardly new or interesting. My relationship with my dad continued to improve with a new season of hockey games, Coke bottles, and his mickeys of gin. Sometimes we even had conversations on the way home. Though we were getting closer, my dad never said he loved me — well, not actually using those words — but for the first time, he was really trying to be a good father. I was inspired to be a better kid.

I was gaining confidence in myself, accepting my family for whom they were. I had a new lease on life playing road hockey, ski racing, roller blading, and idolizing the Canucks. I watched the TV show *Emergency* and dreamt I was one of the firefighters. I felt a lot more positive if I didn't include Mom in any of the picture.

It was nice to feel more 'normal', to look at life differently, more hopefully. When I was younger, hanging out in East Vancouver being a rotten little kid was fun. I liked my friends and when I was with them, everything seemed all right. Now those friends were stealing, smoking pot and drinking. I felt like I was looking in from the outside. I thought about what a little shit I had been as a kid and why my neighbours hated me so much — and I understood. And now that my dad was fully in my life, I didn't want to disappoint him. I wanted him to be proud of me.

Christmas Eve came around, and it was the usual — lots of fighting and yelling. Just before midnight the police arrived. It was surprising they didn't come earlier because that night was a real piece of theatre. Mom and Greg started fighting, then I got into it, and Dad after that. My mom was totally hammered, and a window got broken. Uncle Danny was over, but he'd seen this song and dance before. The two cops who arrived were kind. One tried to get my Mom to go to bed while the other one interrogated my father on the front porch. I didn't know it at the time but this police visit, along with dozens of previous police responses, contributed to our social services file. My mom agreed to go to bed and no one was arrested.

Christmas morning turned out well. Oddly enough, everyone seemed happy. Mom had stuffed our stocking with oranges and candy, I had four presents waiting for me under the tree, and Dad was in a good mood. He had bought a used colour television and we moved our black and white box into the basement. I watched *Nightmare Theater* at midnight on Fridays, *Scooby-Doo* Saturday mornings, *Hockey Night in Canada* with my dad on Saturday nights, and the *Wonderful World of Disney* on Sunday evening. The TV was magical — in colour everything came alive.

It started snowing the next week. All the kids in the neighbourhood went to slide down Williams Lane, the steepest hill around. We built jumps and had competitions to see who could go the fastest. We naturally split into separate groups: the kids from my street, the kids from one street over, and a bunch of scattered kids from all over. We all roughly knew each other, but we didn't really socialize, even going up and down the hill. There was the odd shoving match, and occasionally a few punches got thrown. All in all, it was pretty tame and super fun!

A kid from three streets over was there by himself and he slid down the hill, straight into a drainpipe. He hit it hard and fell into a ditch. Then he just lay there. Kids kept sledding up and down for a long time, maybe twenty or thirty minutes, before anyone went to see what had happened to the kid. Everyone thought he was faking, but when we gathered around him, it looked like he wasn't breathing. We pulled him out of the ditch onto the road and we could see steam coming from his mouth. A kid kicked him hard saying, "Stop faking, get up!" He didn't move and we had no idea what to do.

Eventually, one kid ran home, and after parents called parents, the boy's father showed up. He carried his limp body to his car and I could hear him saying, "Danny, Danny wake up," over and over, and, "I told you to stay away from these kids."

That comment bothered me. *We didn't do anything.* That kid had slid headfirst into the drainpipe on his own. Maybe our reaction time hadn't been the best, but he was lucky we didn't leave him there. Everybody thought he was faking, including me. And he wasn't from our street, so we didn't go out of our way to be helpful.

Danny was in the hospital for a couple weeks and missed months of school. As it turns out, he'd fractured his skull in three places. When he finally came back to school, I apologized, explaining that we had thought he was faking it. He replied that it was okay because he didn't remember anything about that day or after because he'd been in a coma for two weeks before he regained consciousness.

When you're exposed to a traumatic event as a kid, you try to downplay it, whatever it is. It's a coping mechanism. But listening to Danny tell me about how he'd nearly died and the long months of recovery seriously affected me. I realized that life was fragile, it could have been any one of us stuck in a hospital for weeks. We weren't invincible. I thought about some of the stupidly risky things I did as a kid and knew I was lucky (so far) that I had never accidently killed myself or someone else.

After reckoning with my potential mortality, I got into one more fight. It was not in my favour. On the way home from school one day, this random guy came up to me and started pushing me around. I had never seen him before. I was still a skinny little kid who thought he could win by throwing the first punch. I did, and before I knew it the fight was over. He returned a punch right to my throat, and I went down like a bag of dirt. I couldn't breathe and the random guy just walked away. It felt like my Adam's apple was totally crushed. I kept struggling to breathe and had trouble getting up on my feet. I remember thinking, *Thank God the guy didn't keep going.*

It hurt to swallow for days. After that, I had no appetite for fighting.

CHAPTER SIX

Alphatraz

By grade seven, I was in the full swing of puberty — the long, daily showers and obsessive sexual thoughts continued. I had stopped hanging out with Sandra, so for the time being, the chance of me having sex was ruled out. I was still infatuated with my forty-year-old neighbour, and swore my teacher was purposely rubbing against me just to drive me crazy. Erotic dreams plagued my sleep, and on several occasions soaked my sheets.

The winter ski racing season had gone well. I finally had a first-place finish under my belt. Dad and I were watching the Canucks play one of their better seasons.

A new lottery came out — the 6/49—and my father was soon addicted to playing. He would buy a ticket for a dollar. If you got three out of six numbers, you won ten bucks. Four out of six nabbed a couple of hundred, five out of six gave you tens of thousands, and if you netted all six numbers, you were an instant millionaire. But the chance of picking all six correctly were fourteen million to one — in other words, impossible. They would show the winners on TV, and my poor father would be filled with envy. He never missed a draw and would keep track of the winning numbers in a little book he bought. Over the years, he amassed thousands of numbers. I never asked, but I can only assume he was working out some sort of strategy.

I was still happy in my casual classroom with the no desks, split-age group style. That year, we took a class trip to the Strathcona Lodge on Vancouver Island. Initially, my father didn't think he could afford to send me on the trip because our washing machine broke down, and his truck engine had to be rebuilt. When you live paycheck to paycheck, there is only so much money to go around; but by the deadline, Dad somehow came up with the money.

It was one of the most enjoyable school experiences I'd ever had. We canoed, built bonfires, learned about the environment, did our schoolwork outside, and everyone as a class got along well. That field trip seemed like real freedom. Looking at the stars, paddling, and swimming was something I had never experienced. There was so much fun and laughter! It gave me the energy to finish the school year on a positive note.

At first, I thought my father had waited until the last moment to send me on the trip to make me appreciate the opportunity, but I soon realised that my parents were really struggling to pay the bills. I figured it out when my dad wanted to get a better car, but ended up with an old, beat-up van. He was so embarrassed having to drive a piece of crap that broke down constantly. He sometimes had to wait a week until he could pay to get it fixed. It was hard for me to watch him in times like that. He was a proud man. Dad had *one* suit that was almost thirty years old that he would wear for Sunday functions. Then, as if donning a superheroes costume, he was suddenly in his element oozing confidence. It felt good to see him like that. He was a handsome man, and when he was dressed up in that suit he walked with such swagger.

I finished grade seven with two C+'s. I'd never had a C+ before and was so happy. It was the best year I'd had in school yet — there was still hope for me. Despite the good school year, it turned out to be a tough summer. I had a skateboard and one day, skating in the industrial area I lost control, crashing into a 'No Parking' signpost. I separated my shoulder and was in a sling for a month, limiting my ability to play road hockey and shoot the ball.

My old friends were still getting into trouble, breaking into buildings, stealing, sniffing rush and smoking pot. With everything going well with my father and not wanting to let him down, I seriously limited time spent with my friends. Down the lane, my old buddies Darren and Ruutu were stepping up the car part theft. I still had boxes of parts below my deck from past years doing the same thing. I should have gotten rid of them, but I didn't.

Hanging with my younger friend Paulo was one of the best things to happen. He was great for helping me stay out of trouble. He was a good kid. When my shoulder was better, we climbed trees, threw the football, played ball hockey almost every day, and did generally wholesome things. It was a different summer than I was used to and, for the most part, it was free of trouble. We stayed out some nights until the sun came up, throwing rocks at train cars down by the inlet and riding our bikes here and there.

That summer, my mom was away for at least two months in a program to stop drinking, and I stayed out of fights until one August day. I still had my arm in a sling and a group of us were outside my house when three other kids came by. One of them was a guy named Kelly. I knew him, he was younger than me. He and his brother were from the intersection of Georgia and Francis street, and were tough guys. Kelly noticed my arm in a sling and started chirping, asking for a fight. I ignored him. He came over and shoved my injured arm knowing it would be painful; and almost like a reflex, I drilled him in the throat with my healthy right-hand, as hard as I could. He dropped to his knees with his hands around his neck gasping for air: I walked away while he rolled on the ground.

While I didn't get any joy from fighting anymore, that one felt good. The kid deserved it, and my confidence increased. I was on track to surviving the neighbourhood. But while my arm was banged up, I realized how important that ritual exercise of shooting the ball was for my sanity. When you can't move your shoulder, you're incredibly limited in what you can do. I had no way to relieve stress and was constantly on edge. I think part of that stress was from trying so hard to stay out of trouble.

It was the last week of August and the Pacific National Exhibition had come around again. The last big weekend before school started. I was anxious about going into grade eight, my first year of high school. My brother's and sister's good grades were intimidating, and here I was, coming out of learning assistance. I thought if I just kept my head down, stayed out of trouble, and worked hard I would be okay. I was determined to graduate high school, especially since many kids in my neighbourhood never made it through to the final year.

The weeks without Mom around the house were peaceful. There was no fighting, great weather, and the PNE that year was fantastic. I still climbed the fence instead of paying admission — it was nine dollars, and I only had fifteen saved, so even if I wanted to go legally I wouldn't have been able to pay for any of the rides. Like most people who steal, I found a way to justify it. Life couldn't be better. And then, in just a few days, it all unravelled.

I was sitting in my usual perch by the front window. It was Saturday, just before *Hockey Night in Canada*; the Leaf's were playing the Habs and Bob Cole was doing the commentary. As I looked out the window a police cruiser pulled up in front of my house. An officer was walking up to our door.

"Dad," I said, "the police are here."

He got up. "Your goddamn brother is in trouble again," he said.

As he spoke, I saw Darren, my old buddy, lean forward from the back seat of the cop car. My heart sank — I felt instantly nauseated. I ran out ahead of Dad and reached the cop before he made it to the front door. "Collecting car parts, are we?" He blurted out.

I gave Darren the, *I am going to kill you* look, and he slid back out of range.

My dad and the officer found only a couple of boxes under the porch, not all of them, but the look of disgust on my father's face ruined me. I hadn't stolen anything in so long and was really on the path to behaving in better ways. *Why the hell didn't I throw those parts away?* I thought.

While Dad was talking to the officer another cruiser pulled up, and now there were two officers speaking to him. I had no idea what to do, so I did what any kid would. I ran.

I ran all the way up McDonald Street, but before I got to Hastings, Dad pulled up alongside me in his broken-down van. He didn't say a word, just reached over and opened the passenger door.

I got in. The drive home seemed to take hours. When we pulled up, he got out and went into the house. I followed. My father went back to watching TV without saying a word, and I sat there through what felt like the longest game in hockey history.

With about five minutes left in the game, I quietly said, "I'm sorry."

He didn't react. I was waiting for him to pull out his belt and strap me, for the first time in my life, but he didn't move. I felt terrible. I thought he might explode, but I had to keep talking. I said I was sorry again, but he didn't move.

I got up and walked over and stood beside him as he threw back his sixth beer, reclined in his La-Z-Boy, and said, "Dad, I am *so* sorry."

He started to cry. He sat up in his chair and put his head in his hands and started bawling. Then he turned to me, sliding to his knees, and hugged me.

"Boy, they are going to take you away," he sobbed. "Do you understand that they are going to take you away?"

There was a pause, and I came clean, telling him that I was trying to stay out of trouble, that those parts were from years ago, and that I wasn't getting into fights anymore.

He turned and was not crying any longer and said furiously: "You're not allowed to do anything again with those boys down the block, and don't you ever do drugs." He took a breath, and screamed, "Don't *ever* do drugs, you hear me? EVER!"

I was sobbing. He had scared the hell out of me. But I promised him I would never do drugs, that I would be a good person from now on. He got up, went into the kitchen for another beer, and sat down and there were no more words spoken. I waited a bit, then walked away.

I didn't go to the Pacific National Exhibition for the rest of the week.

The next year was for me, the "wonder year" because I'm not exactly sure *how* I survived it. The high school was eleven blocks from my house. Called Alpha, it was one of the toughest schools in greater Vancouver. The local news channel did a report on drugs in district schools and Alpha was at the top of the list for drugs, teachers having sex with students, and a grade eleven student who walked into the nearby 7/11 and shot the clerk in the head with a rifle. The kid was actually a nice guy (I'd heard) — it was bizarre to see him being arrested on the news. A fire burned down a whole wing of the school years before, and of course, a student had started it.

On the school's silver entrance plaque, someone had painted "traz" on the end of the name, spelling out *Alphatraz*. Kids kicked out of other high schools often re-enrolled in Alpha. It was a dysfunctional place, with an eight-foot-high chain-link fence and gates surrounding the grounds. People living near the school joked that the prison-like gates closed from 8:30 am to 3:00 pm to keep the kids in.

The school's reputation was seriously scary but I planned to keep my head down and stay out of trouble. That weekend, I stayed home and didn't hang out with anyone. I played on the street shooting a ball into my hockey net but hardly slept the night before the first day. I was dressed at 7:00 am sharp and sitting at the kitchen table. Mom was still at the detox program, so there was no toast and jam. I wouldn't have eaten it anyway because I was feeling so nervous. It was a twenty-five-minute walk so I left just before 8:00 am. A light rain was falling, which was sort of refreshing as I headed toward the high school. With my army-fatigue backpack wrapped around my shoulder, I thought about the summer.

I'd really started to turn my life around. It was hard not to hang out with the same kids I grew up with, but I did well. Those car parts were from over three years ago, anyway. Halfway to school I decided that the last few days had been the turning point for me — and while I *did* steal all that stuff, I was never charged with theft. I could still make Dad proud and keep everything else in the past.

I arrived at the back entrance of the school. The main entrance lay off Alpha Street, on the other side of Parker Street, but nobody used it because it was on such a busy intersection. In the greeting area there were notices posted for each grade listing every student's name and their class placement. I searched the listings for grade eights but didn't see my name. Luckily, the librarian was nearby and busily answering questions, so I waited my turn to ask. She looked at her list of alphabetically- arranged names and said, "I found you!"

Relief washed over me, until she took me over to a separate bulletin with a large black header that said: Learning Assistance. I felt like throwing up. There I was, thinking I was going to start a new chapter in my life, put into *another* special needs class. No way I would ever make my father proud now, I thought.

I sat through the class with nine other losers. I don't recall a single word the teacher said that day. Clearly, she didn't want to be there either. The first day only went until noon, mainly just so you could meet the teachers. I had one LAC first thing every morning, and then four regular classes: French, English, Social Studies, and one elective. I chose electronics. When that grueling morning was finally finished, I snuck away from the classroom hoping no one would see me.

I noticed a Croatian buddy of mine from elementary school; we hung out every once in a while. He was a great fighter and his mother was Serbian like my dad. He didn't say anything to me when he saw me coming out of the dumb class, but he knew. We walked to our lockers and he asked what I was up to. I said I was just going to head home. I lied, telling him I was grounded and needing to stay out of trouble.

As I walked out, I saw another friend from my elementary school. The sun was out and the brutal morning evaporated lifting me from darkness. As we walked down the steps, a group of about fifty to a hundred kids were starting to gather. The kid beside me said that meant there was going to be a fight. Cool, I thought, I would like to see a high school fight and I had enough time to hang out and watch it happen.

The crowd started to shift — something was definitely occurring. Three guys made their way to the side of the crowd where I was standing. I realised they were clearly striding towards *me*. I turned and started to walk away.

I made it to the parking lot before they jumped me. They were a year or two older, and I had never seen them before. A flurry of punches battered me as I fell to the pavement, and I didn't dare throw any back. As I laid on the ground, one of the guys started kicking me in the groin and chest. A boot smashed my face — I started crying. Panic rushed through me. I rolled and hopped to my feet and started running. It seemed like there were hundreds of people around me, many of them laughing as I sprinted for safety. As I ran out of the school grounds, I could see that the skinny guy who jumped me was right on my ass. I was a great runner, but this guy was catching up *fast*.

I was about half a block away when he tackled me and started beating and kicking. I was crying and blurting out, "What did I do? What did I do?"

"You're not so tough now, are you?" he said. I had no idea what he was talking about, but then he said the name Kelly — the kid I had throttled when my arm was in a sling. Apparently, I caused some damage to his throat when I hit him.

After a few dozen punches and kicks the guy stopped, spit on me and said, "You are a fucking dead man." He walked away and I lay still for a few minutes, then wiped my face and got up and left.

It was the longest walk home ever. I came in the door and went directly to my room. I hoped my dad wouldn't come in. My eye was almost swollen shut, my lip was huge and split, and my ribs were killing me. I couldn't open my left eye, my teeth on the right side of my mouth were sore as hell, and it was hard to breathe. There was this constant dry taste in my mouth — no matter how much water I drank, it would not go away.

I felt like someone had hollowed out my insides. I can't even express how I was feeling except that I honestly wanted to die. My body felt like it weighed about five hundred pounds. I had no energy. There was no way I could face those kids ever again. Everybody had been laughing at me, I would now be the talk of the school. I was the fucking cry-baby who got the shit kicked out of him on day one. My friends would be embarrassed, but worse, if my father knew, he would be ashamed of me. I was humiliated.

I lay on my bed staring at the ceiling and crying. A heavy blanket of hopelessness was covering me. *What am I going to do?* I couldn't go back to school. I didn't want Dad to see me, and certainly didn't want him to know I was back in learning assistance. I recalled the time I ran away from home, attempting to escape my unhappy childhood. Again it became clear that the more I tried to change the more the universe tried to crush me. I was a loser.

My dad was still at work, so I got out of bed and went to the bathroom mirror. My lip and lower chin were layered in a dark reddish bruise. My eye wasn't as swollen, but deeply bloodshot, and there was a big black bruise across the eyelid and cheek. I also saw an ugly kid who looked like a skinny little loser. At that moment I decided the world would be better off without me.

I ran the bathtub, walked into the kitchen, and grabbed one of my mother's fish filleting knives. I remember watching a detective in a Nightmare Theatre show talking about a homicide he was investigating. He said the fastest way to kill yourself was to sit in a warm bath, push a knife through the base of your elbow, and pull it down to your wrist between the radius and ulna bones. You would bleed out in seconds. That was exactly what I was going to do. It was the best option. Mom's filleting knives were extremely sharp, long and skinny. I turned and stared at the bath. Once it was full, I just stood there and looked at it. Finally, I climbed in, crying uncontrollably. I sat there with the knife in my right hand, trying to work up the nerve to push the blade into my arm.

I thought about my dad. He would be so ashamed when people found out his son killed himself. And even though my mom was a drunk, I knew this would finish her off. The neighbours would be thrilled as would those pricks who had kicked the shit out of me. I would be confirming what a loser I really was.

I started sobbing, dropped the knife, and sunk under the water to drown myself. I breathed in through my nose, and the water filled my nasal cavity and flowed into my lungs.

By instinct, I shot out of the bath, involuntarily gasping for air. My body wouldn't let me do it. I lay in the bath until the water got cold, terrified of my future. I didn't have the balls to do it — or deep, deep down, I didn't want to. I didn't know exactly.

But I was still alive.

Thinking it over, I deserved getting the shit kicked out of me. I deserved my family with its dysfunction and alcoholism. Everything I had or did not have in life was my fault — in short, I felt shitty. I wasn't going to be able to change a thing. We had no money and my father's only plan was to win the lottery. I didn't know where my mother was or when she was coming home, and I had no significant relationship with my brother or sister. This was my life. In so many ways I was completely fucked.

The kids at school would laugh at me from now on — and *so what*? I thought. I had a dysfunctional family — *so what*? I didn't care. I decided to face those kids at school and not let them bother me — I didn't give a shit anymore what anyone thought about me. I would take whatever beating and guilt my father was going to lay on me. Most importantly, after coming out of the valley of darkness, I made the decision to live.

CHAPTER SEVEN

Boy at the Bus Stop

My father usually got home around 5:30 pm but I still didn't want him to see me. I went and hid outside, watching the windows of the house. By 9:00 pm, his bedroom light was still on. When it was out, I snuck into the house through the basement. I came up the stairs quietly, grabbed another Coke, bread, and peanut butter — the first time I'd had anything to eat since the beating.

As I lay in bed, I heard my dad's door open and his footsteps crossing the floor to come downstairs. I quickly shut my light off and jumped into bed when he opened the door.

"Steven?"

"Yeah?"

"How's school?"

I didn't answer.

"How was school?"

More silence and Dad turned on the light.

"What is wrong with you? Look at me," he said.

I did, and he showed no reaction while staring at my bruised face.

"Get out of bed and come upstairs," he said and left.

I lay there another few minutes, then got out of bed and walked upstairs.

A year ago, I would not have cared what he said to me, but now I did. When I reached the top of the stairs, I heard him crack a beer, and sink into his chair. I walked into the living room and sat slumped on the couch looking at the floor. I sat there uncomfortably until Dad started talking.

He took a swig of his beer, looked at me for a bit and then said, "I know I have failed at many things as a father, but I thought I taught you how to fight."

I was trying to think of how I could explain my side of the story, why I couldn't return to that school, but he just kept talking. He ranted on about his past fights and how he'd always gotten the upper hand with his highly technical "punch them right in the nose technique."

After what seemed like an hour he said, "I want you to start boxing," and took another pull on his beer. He didn't say anymore and continued watching TV.

With that, I went downstairs and flopped down on my bed. I knew there was no sense trying to explain that three guys had kicked the shit out of me with no way to escape. Dad would have thought of me as weak but I knew there was more to come when I returned to that school. I decided to do whatever my father wanted but was terrified to go back to school. I skipped the entire first week.

On Saturday, my father declared he was taking me to my new boxing club. We drove down to Main and Hastings, one of the toughest areas of Vancouver's east side. We parked the truck on Main Street across the street from the police station. As I tried to open the door, a couple of wasted people were in the way, yelling and staggering around. When I managed to get out of the truck, Dad was well ahead of me. I ran to catch up and as we turned the corner onto Hastings there were dozens of people sleeping, smoking, and making moaning sounds right in the middle of the sidewalk. It was like something out of a movie, like "The Walking Dead." I wasn't exactly sure why we were in this part of town until I saw the sign: *Inter City Athletic Centre, Shamrock Boxing Club.*

We walked through the front door and past two guys sparring in a huge boxing ring. I didn't know a lot about boxing but it looked super cool — lots of guys skipping and hitting bags — I was excited to get started. My dad asked to see Mr. Pollock and I stood there in my baggy blue jeans and a Vancouver Whitecaps t-shirt with my blackened left eye and ribs that were still sore.

I could see my father talking to a terrifying man. That man walked over and barked, "Steven, come with me!" Dad told me to take the bus home, gave me thirty cents for the fare, and walked out of the gym. I ran to catch up with Mr. Pollock and followed him downstairs to a wet stinking dungeon. I could hear showers running and locker doors banging. Guys wandered around in towels and posters of naked women covered the walls.

Mr. Pollock told me to change into my workout gear and I said, "I didn't bring any." He then yelled at me in front of the other tough convict-looking guys, "What do you mean? Well, whatever ... Grab a skipping rope!" I picked a rope off the floor by the lockers and followed Mr. Pollock as he headed up the stairs.

He turned around and said, "Your father says you don't know how to fight, so he wants you to box. Listen to me kid, if you are going to come to this club you are going to work your ass off, and listen to everything I tell you, got it?"

"Okay," I nervously blurted out.

"Skip for thirty minutes and then do four sets of twenty-five sit ups," he said.

I found a corner and started skipping. After a couple of minutes I had to stop. I started over then had to stop again. *Holy fuck, this is hard,* I thought, but I was terrified of this Mr. Pollock dude. *I will just keep doing it like this until he says something.* After twenty minutes of skipping, I felt like dying — my shirt and jeans were full of sweat.

Mr. Pollock walked up and said, "There is a drinking fountain over by the ring. Go get a drink and come back and do four sets of twenty-five sit ups." He was still there when I came back after slurping down a gallon of water. I lay down in front of him and started doing sit ups. They were easier to do than the skipping, but my ribs were really hurting me. When I came into the last part of the crunch, Mr. Pollock stopped me after doing about forty. He could clearly see me grimacing.

"Do push-ups until I say stop," he said and walked away again.

I was struggling with the push-ups — my ribs were now burning. I was compensating and doing short little lifts, and from across the gym Mr. Pollock yelled, "Steven get that ass down — keep your body straight when you are doing those!"

Oh my god, that makes it so much harder, I thought. My skinny little arms were shaking uncontrollably as if they might explode. I collapsed on the ground and weakly tried to do a few more.

Mr. Pollack came up to me and said, "You're done. I want you back here every Saturday, Tuesday and Thursday, got it?" I nodded and he walked away yelling at a big guy sparring in the ring to keep his left hand up when he was throwing jabs.

I walked out soaking wet with sweat. I bobbed and weaved my way through the drug addicts sitting on the pavement in front of the boxing club. By the time I got to the bus stop, half a block away, I sat down feeling exhausted and stunned yet strangely peaceful. My bus, the number 14 Hastings, pulled up within minutes, but I didn't get on. I can't explain it, but sitting there surrounded by drug addicts, and people with all kinds of problems, a calm come over me. I had never felt like that before and relished the moment. Fifteen minutes later, the next bus pulled up. I got on and sat in the very back. Even though I was sore, stinky and wet, I felt okay about me. That bus ride home was one I will never forget. I thought about so many things: school, my father, and attempting to take my own life a few days before. For the first time, it seemed, I was thinking clearly.

I didn't do much that weekend, my ribs were sore so I just watched TV. For some reason my father never said a word to me, but he didn't seem angry, just really quiet.

In hindsight, it seems obvious that my father did the right thing sending me to the boxing club and back to school. Something had shifted in my head. I was on the road to becoming a boxer and staying out of trouble, doing everything it took to be good and making something of my life. Just one week before, I hated life and wanted to die. I'm certain a part of me *did* die. Maybe that is what it took to gain a newfound sense of courage and hopefulness for the future.

When I returned to high school, I was taunted daily by a group of four to six guys. They would randomly attack, punching or pushing me down. I would open my locker unaware that one of these losers was walking up to me, throwing a blind punch that knocked me down to the floor. I was always watching over my shoulder, but after a while, I accepted it was going to happen. I began to enjoy boxing more, dreaming about fighting back — but I never did. I just cowered, having been so humiliated by my beating in the parking lot.

I was still in LAC and my father was *not* thrilled, but he allowed me to start playing ice hockey that year. I was still boxing, and enjoyed the sport but in the boxing club, I always kept my head down. I didn't really like the neighbourhood with guys buying heroin and shooting up in the entrance to the club. It was a seriously tough area.

At the same time, I was happy waiting for the bus. Sitting at that bus stop letting one or two go by without getting on, was a special time for me, a way of clearing my head.

Going to and from the boxing club, I did get to know a few of the homeless people. Some would tell me their stories. Judy had three kids and worked in a fashion store until her husband left her and she went from using pain medication to cocaine then heroin. John was a guy who waved to me every time he saw me. I always made a point of going over and shaking his hand. I felt bad for those folks. They were so nice and I wished I could help them in some way. Sadly, Judy just disappeared one day, like many do - lost to an overdose or jail.

One Sunday we went to a swap meet and bought used hockey equipment and Dad registered me to play. I was really excited about it. Boxing and hockey were a great mix of sports, going hand in hand. I couldn't skate at all, I'd never done it before, but I'd been playing street hockey for a long time, so my hand-eye coordination was good. All the other kids had been playing on ice for years so I was a real greenhorn, but I didn't care. I adored the sport and to me, the coolest part was that you could fight in hockey. My boxing techniques came in handy to fuel the rage I felt from the pent-up frustration of getting pushed around at school. Both my coaches that year were RCMP police officers, and they saw me as a kid who could barely play hockey, but when it came to tangling on the ice, I fought with a smile on my face. Even though I was the skinniest player on the team, I would skate straight down the ice, drop my shoulder, and hit kids in the open ice, and they would go flying. Then, if they wanted to fight, I was down for that too. I didn't speak much, making my coaches think of me as a strangely polite kid. They would burst out laughing when I rocked players on the other team. Cheering whenever I hit someone, my teammates seemed to enjoy having this quiet and brutal skater riling up the opposing teams.

After the game, in the dressing room, I would not say a word pulling off my gear and then leaving. I did the same thing every game and didn't make any friends that first year. There was no one from Alphatraz on that team, and I think everyone was trying to figure me out. The team respected me for being a first-year player who couldn't skate but went out there hitting everything that moved. When I scored my first goal halfway through the season, my bench went crazy.

My father came out to every game and practice. After each game I would get the same speech. "Son, when you hit a kid like that," Dad would say, "bring your body from a crouched position into a straight, extended position just as you hit him." He was one of those fathers who was an immediate expert on anything and everything. Though he never played sports, his technique was bang on — no other kid was hitting like that. It gave me a surge of confidence on the ice, blasting kids left and right. It was simple and fun. After each impressive hit, I would turn to the stands and look at my dad. Even from the ice, I could see a massive smile on his face.

One day after a brutal workout at the boxing club, I was sitting at my favourite spot - the bus stop at Main and Hastings on Vancouver's east side, and something magical happened. Fire Engine #2 rolled up to the intersection and I was watching from only a few hundred feet away. When they drove by, a firefighter in the back looked straight at me and gave me a smile. I smiled back. He looked so cool. As they drove off into the distance, I decided, then and there, that I wanted to be a firefighter. I didn't care how hard the schooling might be - I was going to be just like that cool guy who had smiled at me. I never forgot that moment of epiphany.

My mom finally came home from rehab and looked awful. She was not drinking but was definitely on edge with very bad shakes. She and my father did not speak at all. I felt bad for her and tried to talk to her as much as I could, but it was hard for me to see her in such a state.

By the end of the hockey season, the coaches loved me, even though I had only two goals under my belt, and the second one had bounced, hit me on the ass and went in. I got the "Most Exciting Player" award that first year. The proceedings were voted on by the entire team. Overall, it made for an awesome year.

Unfortunately for my father, it was a tough year. Mom went back to drinking heavily, staggering around every night, falling and hurting herself, screaming, shouting and prompting several police visits. Then, without notice, my father lost his job. The washing machine completely broke down, and already behind on last month's mortgage payment, he wasn't able to buy a new one. He became seriously depressed and started drinking more.

Dad had loved his job with the Surrey School Board working as a dry-waller in the maintenance department. He was laid off while I was playing hockey, but the games were a big deal for both of us. My dad was happy watching his son play and I enjoyed listening to him talk about 'hitting like this' or 'shooting like that' on the drive home. The guy had never played a damn sport, but there he was coaching me on the finer details of the game. I loved it when he did that. It seemed the bad things I had done when I was younger were fading from his mind, but as soon as he got home, back to my mother, he just put his head down and drank.

Dad seemed to be giving up on everything. It is hard to see someone you love going downhill, especially when you're only thirteen. I didn't have those same feelings for my mom, though. When she was depressed and got loaded, she turned into an evil bitch.

My dad frequently watched my games from the bar in the sports complex. After losing his job, being in a bar was not a good mix because he got really drunk. Going home after one game, he was pulled over and charged with "Driving Under the Influence" and arrested.

This kick-started an event that would be the end of our family. We were already a target of the Ministry of Family Services and Child Protection, and my father had warned me if I kept getting into trouble, they were going to take me away. Well, with my mom drinking again, the police showing up to our home, and my jobless father getting an impaired charge, a big problem was brewing.

Dad initially hired a big-name lawyer, Harry Rankin, to fight the impaired charge. Eventually Rankin represented my father in a dispute with Child Protection. One day Dad took me to the lawyer's office. It was in the same tough part of town, Vancouver's East side, just a few blocks from the boxing club.

Mr. Rankin was really nice when he talked with me one-on-one for a couple of hours while a secretary furiously wrote down every word I said. When I first sat down in the office, I assumed that I was helping my dad get out of the impaired charge, but the questions were mostly about my mom and the written statements made in past police responses. I found that strange. The last question asked was, "Who would it be, if you could pick only one of your parents to live with?"

Right away I answered, "My father."

The lawyer asked me to wait outside and after talking with my dad for another hour, we headed home. The next day we returned to Rankin's office and after talking with my dad privately, I was asked to come in and sign something called an affidavit, a legal document to confirm that what I said was true.

It was a lot of papers, but I signed and the lawyer walked over to me and put his hand on my shoulder and said, "Steven, we are going to do everything we can to help your father, and what your father needs you to do is to stay out of trouble and try and get your grades up. Can you do what he asked?"

Without hesitating, I said, "Yes."

When I wasn't playing sports, I hung out with Paulo. Honestly, that kid didn't have a bad bone in his body, and it really helped me stay out of trouble. We were always throwing or shooting a ball; I don't remember a single day that year that we didn't do *something* with a ball. Most of my buddies were still fooling around with pot and snorting rush. I still hung out with them once in a while, but never did the drugs, and neither did Paulo.

Eventually, I told my father I didn't want to box anymore, and he just said, "Okay, pick another sport." I chose lacrosse. It was obvious Dad felt that if he kept me in sports, I would keep out of trouble, and he was right, for the most part.

My father losing his job scared the hell out of me. Those weeks of him not having money to buy his beer, or even put gas in the car, was a wake-up call for me. I was not sure what a lawyer like Harry Rankin cost, but it was likely expensive. I decided to get a job.

Dad did find another job as a janitor. It gave him a cheque to pay the bills, but he hated it with a passion and was still depressed, if not more so.

Toward the end of the summer, the cannery my mom worked for was looking for someone to quality check the line, so I went down and applied. You had to be sixteen to work there, so I lied on the application. They took away the paper, gave me a smock, and I was working that same day. I was suddenly making huge money — thirteen dollars per hour. While it took three buses to get to the job, about two hours each way, for that kind of money I had no complaints commuting.

The Pacific National Exhibition was on again. We climbed the fence and rode the rides for three straight days — it was awesome. Paulo didn't like rides but I forced him to go on the sky-swing — a kind of merry-go-round that spins about fifty feet off the ground. He begged me, but I demanded we go, and halfway through the ride he shouted that he was going to throw up. I started laughing until suddenly he did. All over me. He covered me, and then, in his perfectly clean clothes, smiled and said, "This ride is not so bad!"

I went home because every fly in the park was feeding off me. You could smell me from twenty feet away.

CHAPTER EIGHT

Gone, Gone, Gone ...

After the PNE, school started up again. An amazing thing happened for grade nine. They forgot to put me in learning assistance. For the first time in years, I had a regular class schedule. Several kids from LAC came up and asked me where I had gone, they wanted to know how I managed to get out. Unlike me, they liked it because those classes were just a way to get through high school.

I hated the stigma of the special classes and what it meant to my dad, but I was terrified that I wouldn't be able to get through regular classes. I didn't have to retake French, even though I failed it. I could finally take the classes I wanted, so I took drafting and woodworking. I was nervously excited about grade nine. The eighth grade had been a blur. I wanted to forget about it and move on.

My locker was one of the few in the basement. Other students hated having lockers down there, but I loved it — the goon squad that roughed me up on a regular basis wouldn't come by because it was too far out of the way

September flew by and the regular hockey season got underway. I was thrilled as I had practiced my skating every day over the summer and had vastly improved. The downside was that my dad couldn't drive me to games and practices anymore. His new janitorial job had him working nights and early mornings. Sometimes he would drop me off at the rink at 5:30 in the morning for my 6:30 practice then I would take three buses home, drop off my gear, and walk the eleven blocks to school. I didn't mind it at all. Dad still hated his job but was not as depressed. I looked forward to him coming to watch me at weekend games. I just loved doing something big on the ice and then looking up at him.

My mom came to one of my games loaded. It was embarrassing seeing people move away from her in the stands. One guy on the team picked her out and asked whose mom it was. I ignored him and didn't answer. She never came again but that one time could have turned out very badly.

I was asked to try out for a Rep B team that September. I was super nervous about it and everything else seemed unimportant. The tryout was over a weekend, stretched across two days.

The coaches had the teams pretty much picked, but they'd heard tales about this skinny tall kid that liked to hit everything that moved. The other thing I had developed, mostly from playing street hockey, was a good wrist shot. I would pull it *way* back, then release. It was pretty accurate, right on point and coupled with my improved skating maybe I had a slim chance. The other guys had been in camps and skating clinics, likely from the age of five or younger. Skating and hockey are expensive sports and there was no way my dad could afford it. These were tough days financially — we still had the broken van and no dishwasher — I felt terrible for him. I made great cash at the cannery and though he wouldn't take any from me, at least I never had to ask him for money.

The tryouts were three hours each day. I arrived at 9:00 am on Saturday and was immediately intimidated. I didn't know anyone. These kids were all much bigger than the ones I usually played with. Once we got out onto the ice, I saw how fast and fluid their skating strides were compared to my choppy, lanky style. I struggled through the drills while the other kids breezed through them. I had trouble taking a pass because they were hit so hard, and I couldn't time it properly. In the last hour, we had a scrimmage — I didn't try to hit anyone — to be honest, they were so agile and fast I couldn't even catch them. They were on a completely different level.

They hit me though. I got rocked often, having to pick myself up off the ice several times for having my head down and not being quick enough to dodge. Even though the tryouts went for two days, one of the coaches came up to me on that Saturday as I was taking my gear off and said, "Sorry pal, it's not going to work. Come again next year and give it a shot." The guy told me that in the packed dressing room, *right* in front of a whole bunch of kids I didn't know. You could hear a pin drop. I was mortified. I finished taking off my gear and walked out to the parking lot where my dad waited.

I got into the car and he said, "Don't worry son, it takes a day to get your bearings. You'll do better tomorrow."

I waited a couple of minutes and then said, "I'm not coming back tomorrow."

He didn't say a word, didn't look at me, we just drove. I felt bad about all the equipment, all the money spent, and Dad more excited about this tryout than I was. When we got home, he just grabbed a beer and sat in his chair.

After the episode in the dressing room, I was angry, but rather than feel sorry for myself, I decided to face the issue head on. By practicing every Saturday, Sunday and sometimes after school, I was determined to improve my skating skills. Now I took the hockey drills seriously, focusing on long pushes and wide crossovers.

By the time Christmas came around I was a far better skater. I asked my dad if I could take some lessons with a power skater and he immediately said yes. Skating is key in the game of hockey and when you become a strong skater, everything else falls into place.

On my way home one afternoon, the goon squad from school singled me out. The four of them grabbed me and I took a few shots to the head but walked away as they called me a bunch of low-life names. I just accepted it and tried to put it out of my head. I had learned how to get a better grip on my emotions — not to turn them on and off at will, but to hold them in better.

Christmas had arrived, and it was another doozy. The front window got broken, and Mom was cut but no one knew how badly because she bandaged it up right away. She kept telling everyone it was terrible but I was pretty sure it was no big deal.

A week later, Mom was gone again. Dad said she went away to get help in some sort of rehab facility. The house was silent, and it felt strange, but doing my homework was so much easier when it was quiet. The kitchen wasn't filled with Mom's cigarette smoke, and no voice was screaming at me.

One night, doing my homework in the kitchen, I could hear scratching. I turned and looked at the lower cabinet and there was this little mouse trying to open the door. We had tons of mice in our house. I could hear them running through the vents at night. I was so used to it that it never bothered me. I remember thinking if I could hear mice, it meant the fighting had stopped. As a kid, it was a comforting sound.

"Quiet, huh?" I said to the mouse. He looked at me then scurried away.

Hockey was going well and school was as good as it ever was. I was never going to be a great student, but I was now getting C's on average. January was memorable because of how peaceful my home was. My sister was leaving for Simon Fraser University and my brother was already going to the University of British Columbia, both prestigious schools.

I started my second term of math with a new teacher named Mr. Heinz. He was not the most likable guy at school and he was well-known to be a tough marker. The first day he came up to me and said, "Mr. Serbic, I am excited to have you in my class. Your brother was one of the most intelligent students this school has ever seen, and your sister maintained that standard — I have high hopes for you to do the same." My brother and sister got straight A's with him *every year* they had him. After my first test result, he stopped talking to me. I'm not joking — he never spoke to me again for the rest of the year. I got a C- as a final grade, and the funny thing was I was super happy with that mark.

I played a hockey tournament in January and received "Most Valuable Player" for scoring a whack of goals and laying out some massive hits. The Rep B team ended up calling me in for a couple of games that year and I performed well — not fantastic, but not out of place. If they gave me a chance, I was certain I could play a whole season at that level with no problem.

After a month or so, my mom came home. She looked awful and wouldn't talk about her stay in rehab. She returned to the cannery and started going to a support group. It was a tense time in our home. We were all rooting for Mom but she was invisible — never home. She was depressed and looked run down. It was hard to watch, but at least she was sober and that was what mattered.

About three weeks later, we got into a massive fight as I left for a hockey game. I was getting picked up by another family and as I walked out the door, I remember thinking that I didn't care anymore, maybe she was better as a drunk. I didn't mean it; I was just angry.

When I came home from hockey that night, there was Mom at the kitchen table, absolutely hammered. I remember that moment well. I felt entirely responsible because the fight we had was so unnecessary. I didn't say a word, nor did she as I walked by. It was a moment when I knew I needed to figure out a plan for my own life. I wanted to have a positive effect on others, not a negative one. I wanted to run away again, but I couldn't do that to my dad — he would be devastated and lonely if I wasn't there for him.

I had a fight with my mother when she was at her weakest, just hanging on, and it was *that* fight that pushed her over the edge, got her back on the bottle. In hindsight, I could have handled it so many ways, but instead, I decided to fight. I will never forget that decision; it was cowardly of me, and there was no taking it back. The rehab and the confidence my mother was working towards was gone. We were all right back to where we were before, and I was totally responsible. It was a very shitty few weeks for me after that because I couldn't change what had happened, and the knowledge of my hand in it consumed me.

Thankfully, I had hockey in my life to take my mind off everything. I began to think that maybe I could get good enough to play professionally someday. Yeah, I know, every kid thinks that, but I wasn't thinking of it as a way to become rich and famous. To me, it was a way out, a door to happiness. I liked dreaming about it—the skating, the game, and all the skill sets it offered and demanded from a struggling kid like myself. It seemed like the perfect fit.

My brother and sister weren't around much, spending most of their time at their respective universities, so most of the fighting surrounded my mother and father and, occasionally, me.

One Saturday night, I had plans to go over to a buddy's house and play foosball, drink a few beers, and go downtown. I wasn't feeling good about myself. I was angry about the previous fight with my mom, and how much I hated her when she was drunk. My friends never came over to my house because I didn't invite them. That night, my mother was already loaded at

5:00 pm and I was planning to leave by 6:00. I couldn't get out of there fast enough. As I was getting dressed, I could hear a conversation upstairs. Mom was talking loudly as people do when they are really loaded. I started up the stairs to the kitchen and heard a couple of my buddies in the kitchen talking to my mom. She was staggering drunk and shouting at them, "What the hell are you doing here?" When I came into the kitchen she yelled, "There he is!" My buddies could see how ashamed I was of my mother. I motioned for them to head out the door.

As I walked past, Mom lunged, trying to grab me. I dodged, and she missed. I quickly pushed my buddies, saying, "Let's go," trying to get out of there. As I grabbed my shoes, Mom said, "Where do you think you're going?" I didn't answer and put on my shoes. She said it again and grabbed me. My friends were in the laundry room, standing by the back door. I pushed her off and started to walk away. Before I knew it, she tried to tackle me, wrapping her arms around my neck, and leaping onto my back. I fell to the ground at the doorway of the laundry room and yelled in panic for my buddies to leave. I pushed her off again, got to my feet and so did she. She came at me again, and I did one of the most regrettable things I have ever done in my life.

She ran at me, slurring something, and went into attack mode. I turned around and with built up rage toward her, shoved with everything I had. She went flying in the air backwards and went down, *hard*, whacking her head on the ground where she fell. She was crying, and just lay there with no movement — just moaning and kind of rolling around. Then she started screaming that her back was broken and I was in shock standing there. It was a real low point for me — I had physically struck my mother.

My friends left without saying a word, but they could hear her screaming as they exited the yard.

I don't know where it came from. I had just reacted, like a scared animal. I felt so terrible. I went back inside telling her repeatedly, "Your back is not broken, I'm so sorry." She just lay there, crying and cursing at me. After what seemed like an hour, I helped her up and managed to get her into bed.

I went to my bedroom and lay on the floor. I cried like I'd never cried before — I had just assaulted my own mother — I was furious with myself. A couple of days later, one of my friends who had been there told me if I ever needed a place to stay, I could come to his house. I said thanks and walked away quickly; I was choking up, starting to cry.

That was the first time that anyone outside our home, aside from the neighbours, had any idea what was going on. I stopped speaking to my mom entirely — I mean not a word. I was always feeling shame when I saw her. She brought it up all the time when she was loaded, "You going to hit your mother again, tough guy?" or, "Who beats up their own mother?" She was right, I thought, *Who the fuck does that*?

Those following months were humbling. Just making eye contact with my mom made me feel guilty. The house had an even more brutal, oppressively negative vibe to it than before. The mice and even rats were suddenly everywhere — it was disgusting.

To top it off, my father was going down to the lawyer's office every week now. I was certain *something* big was about to drop.

I sunk back into depression, dwelling on all the negatives in my life: my mother the drunk, the thugs making my life miserable at school, and living in that shitty little house on the corner of Napier and McDonald.

I finished up the hockey season on the top line of the best team in the House division and had been called up for several games to play on the Rep B team — all in all, the season could not have gone better.

I started playing lacrosse that spring even though I had never held a stick before. It was awkward, totally different from a hockey stick. I went to tryouts and, fortunately for me, they didn't have enough players trying out, so I made the team by default. I loved the game, and it was only a two-month season. During the lacrosse season, my buddy Rich asked if I wanted to play football, which sounded fine to me.

In the spring of ninth grade, I was playing lacrosse and football for the Renfrew Trojans, both big hitting contact sports. I was terrible at the finesse points of lacrosse, but the coach loved me because I would chase down their biggest player and use every ounce I had to smash into him. I discovered how to use my skinny body as leverage, figured out where to plant my feet just as I was about to hit, and I could send people flying. The best part about it was that no one was intimidated by me on the lacrosse court, so when I trotted towards them and then suddenly charged last minute, they were totally caught off guard. I just loved this new sport, and my dad would come and watch the games.

Football was a different story. The coach had me as both a tight end and left receiver. I could run like the wind and practiced catching the ball constantly, so I was ready to play. On the first play of my very first game against the Surrey Bears, I caught a pass from the quarterback on our own forty-yard line and ran it in for a touchdown.

I started the season well but ended up getting on the coach's bad side. I didn't see a lot of throws for the rest of the season, but since I played both ways, as a tight end and left receiver, I played a lot.

Unfortunately, I suffered two big concussions that year. I played through one, but it affected me for months. I finished lacrosse and while there was lots of contact in that sport, the constant headache from my concussion didn't seem to get any worse. I did have dizzy, blurry spells and for some reason, a sore stomach.

I was busy that summer with sports and working at the cannery. I just wanted to stay out of the house. My mother was barely working, drunk every day, and it was brutal to be at home. When I didn't have a game or a practice, I would play road hockey out on the corner or with my buddy Paulo.

Lacrosse season ended, and football finished up shortly after. I continued to work at the fish cannery. Even though my mother worked at the same place, we rarely saw each other and *never* spoke, not one word. It was awkward — I don't think anyone there knew we were family. On days off, I went to the rink to skate. I would stay all day, skating for eight hours from opening to closing. Sometimes it was just me and five pucks that I would shoot to my heart's content. I was excited to return to tryouts and see if I could make that Rep team.

I quit boxing that summer because I wanted to concentrate on hockey, football, and lacrosse. Don't get me wrong, I enjoyed the boxing training, but the gym and the people in it were creepy. Half the guys working out in there were hardened criminals and outside the street drug scene freaked me out. Going there several times a week changed me. So did the commute. Walking that half-block on Vancouver's toughest street was educating. I got to know many homeless people and druggies. They all had stories to tell — sad and fascinating at the same time. Walking the streets of the East side with nothing but bus fare in my pocket and talking to people who only wanted money for drugs put me in a tight spot. I could only talk and could not give them money. When they realized I had no money, they accepted me for conversation alone. Some of them were former executives, bankers, professional athletes, who now lived for using drugs.

I had discovered their vibrant homeless community. They truly cared about each other. I would ask about someone I had met, like where Mary or George was, and the homeless person would tell me, shedding tears, that they were gone. People would overdose regularly but were too addicted or too low to fight their way out of the lifestyle. The East Side was (and still is) the final pitstop for thousands of addicts. I really cared for some of them. My father used to say their situation was their own fault, but hearing their stories, I learned that wasn't always the case.

It helped me feel for my mom. She was no different from those addicts, except that she had a family and a home to go to. I understood for the first time how hard it must have been for her.

But Mom was as bad as ever. Any improvement she made in the rehab centre wore off quickly — it was coming home to us that set her off. I have no idea what my mom wished for from life. She was complicated, always saying how wonderful everything was when she was sober, and then when she was pissed, screaming about how brutal everything was. I hated and loved, with all my heart, the bipolar, alcoholic woman that my mother was.

That summer, I felt less of a loser. Passing grade nine and playing sports helped me gain confidence, and apart from the constant concussion headache that I couldn't shake, I felt strong and hopeful.

I left the cannery at the end of the summer and got a job cleaning tables in McDonald's in the first week of September. The restaurant was right down the street from Alphatraz and was constantly busy serving high school kids. I was a little intimidated at first, but I just put my head down and worked. I knew everyone that came in from the high school. They were always chatting me up but I still worked my ass off. This, however, did not sit well with the manager. He didn't like me knowing half of the customers and was frustrated that he couldn't bust me for talking.

Then hockey started and I gave the manager my schedule for games and practices. He told me to choose between hockey or McDonalds. There was no way he was going to work around everyone else's schedules *just* so I could play hockey. I asked him if I could be put on-call, part-time, taking me off the schedule entirely. He said no, though it was done for all the university students. So I went over his head and asked the regional manager, who said that it was no problem, and for me to consider it done. Well, when my manager found out, he came up to me fuming. He told me I'd better assume my life was going to be a living hell because he would give me every shit shift available.

And he did.

I learned to hate McDonald's — not the work itself, but I absolutely despised that manager, who went out of his way to make my life difficult on every single shift. My McDonald's career was short-lived. Although it paid far less than my former job at the cannery, I liked the social side of it. In fact, if that damn manager had cut me some slack, I could have probably worked there happily for the rest of high school. But there was no way he was going to let that happen. During one shift it finally came to a head.

I was cleaning tables and a girl from school that I had a major crush on, walked in. She noticed me and came over to say hi — she was genuinely happy to see me. It was all awesome until the manager saw me talking and screamed at me from the back to get to work, only to embarrass me. So, I thought *fuck it*, and ignored him. After about five more minutes talking with her, I could see out of the corner of my eye the manager walking towards me. Before I could react, he dumped a five-gallon pail of lettuce on me. The girl burst out laughing and walked away.

My manager smiled and said, "Next time you decide to use selective hearing, don't forget I'm paying you to clean this shit up!" and stalked off.

I almost charged into his office. It was all I could do to hold back my rage. I was shaking uncontrollably and had to go outside to cool off. I seriously wanted to kill him, to beat him to death. It was a vision so visceral and real that I had to walk out.

This incident happened on a night shift. Usually at shift close, I would walk around the parking lot and pick up all the garbage. I was still in shock and furious about the lettuce incident, so I lingered in the parking lot a bit longer. That manager was twice the size of me, so there was no way I would get in a fight with him because I'd probably get killed. But I was so enraged, pacing around the parking lot picking up trash for a long time. Hours later, I still didn't have my emotions under control.

The manager drove a fully restored custom Chevy Impala, and I vehemently hated it because it was his — but honestly, it was a spectacular car. He parked it clear across the parking lot near the dumpsters so nobody would get near it and dent the doors or something. It was his baby, and it was in mint condition.

In a fit of pique, I dumped my bag of garbage on top of his car. Then I jumped inside the dumpster and proceeded to throw garbage from the bin onto his car. It was a violent resurgence of that one big problem I had — the inability to stop myself from following through with what I knew was a bad idea. I unloaded every single piece of garbage out of that dumpster onto his mint Chevy Impala.

It took about fifteen minutes. When I was finished, his car wasn't visible under the mound of garbage. I got my rusty banana seat bike and went around to the front of the restaurant where I could see the manager working at the till. I pounded on the door until I got his attention. He responded by screaming, "What do you want?"

"I want you to go fuck yourself!" I shouted back. "And go look at your car, asshole."

And I rode away. The next day, the police arrived at my house, and my dad was not impressed. I'd been officially fired and the manager wanted the police to press vandalism charges against me. He also wanted to collect damages that were apparently done to his car from the garbage.

When I told my dad the whole story, he was totally supportive. It was the first time in my life that my dad had my back *after* I had done something really stupid. He told me he would have done exactly the same thing and was proud of me. I was blown away when he said that.

What I didn't understand was that incident and the police contacting my father set something off with Social Services — some kind of final straw between our family and the ministry. Over the month that followed, my father went to and from the lawyers. I kept asking him what was going on, but he hemmed, hawed, and never told me.

One day we went together to Harry Rankin's law office at Main and Hastings. We sat down and Rankin asked, "How're you doing today?" I said I was okay. Then he asked if I knew why we were there. I had a pretty good idea of what was happening. "The Ministry of Social Services is looking to move me to another home, isn't it?" I blurted out.

Harry looked at my dad and said, "Well, not exactly — but if we don't do some things right now, that's exactly what will happen. Your dad loves you. He thinks you have so much potential, but your family has been found unfit to raise their own children. You're the only minor left in your home, and you have a bit of a troubled history."

I said I had been doing better staying out of trouble. "I know exactly why you're telling me this, and I really want to live with my father."

"That's exactly what I needed to hear," Harry replied. "Okay," he said, "let's get busy."

I spent a couple of hours making statements for Harry and his assistant, signing affidavits, and at the end of the meeting he looked at my father and said, "I think we have everything we need. Let's see what happens."

That next week, the house was eerily quiet. My dad avoided my mother entirely.

Then, out of the blue, two RCMP officers and a woman from Social Services showed up at the door, asking to speak with my mother. They asked her to come outside and talk with them, but she refused. She stayed sitting at the kitchen table crying. They entered the house and showed her a bunch of paperwork. She laughed and said, "This is my house, and *I am not going anywhere!*"

The RCMP officer said if she didn't get up, they would have to remove her. I was standing there, stunned. I knew what was happening but was in total shock. Mom started screaming how my father had been plotting and planning this for a long time and that she worked every day to pay for this house. She was adamant about not leaving and then rolled up her pant legs showing the police officers her varicose veins, screaming, "Look, look what he's done to me! He ruined my life and now you're trying to take me away from my home?" She looked right at me and screamed, "How could you do this to me?"

I hung my head, walked to my room and lay on the bed. I could hear the police trying to remove her and Mom fighting back. Things were breaking. I started to cry.

The Social Services woman spoke to my mom as the police officers restrained her. She told her that under the Court of Canada's Social Services Act (or something like that) she was being removed from the premises to preserve the safety of a child. I could hear her crying, "Please don't do this, please don't do this1" As she was being removed, Mom kept screaming, "Don't forget I love you, Steven, I have always loved you!"

I heard the screen door close, so I got up. The Social Services woman was in my mom's room. She was grabbing clothing and other items and I asked her what was going to happen to my mom. She looked at me and said sternly, "You need to stay out of trouble, do you understand?" I nodded but didn't say another word.

The Social Services woman left, and the house was totally quiet. My mother never saw the inside of our home again.

CHAPTER NINE

The Best and Worst Day of My Life

It's funny, the things you don't notice when you're a kid, or that you choose not to. Apparently, there had been a flurry of social service enquiries for some time, and my father had been doing damage control for the last couple of years. In my mind, that explained the increase in his drinking around that time. His lawyer, Harry Rankin, cost a lot of money and Dad mentioned once that he would be paying Harry for the rest of his life. Rankin had been holding off the Ministry of Social Services for quite some time. He advised my father to be sure I stayed out of trouble and improved my grades to show that life was more positive in this new environment. The whole effort was to keep us together.

My father was the toughest man I've ever met. He had an angry stare that could kill. One day he walked in the door after work and asked if everything was okay with me. I said yeah, it's good, but he was not in a very good mood for some reason.

"Are you sure?" he asked angrily.

"Yes, I'm sure."

He grabbed a beer, flopped onto the La-Z-Boy and didn't say another word. I thought it was strange but found out later that one of the neighbours had something stolen out of their yard. They called the police and told them it was me. It wasn't me but I had a good idea of who it was. I realized that, having been a little shit, no matter what I did going forward in some people's eyes, I would always be a rotten kid. Once a shit-rat, always a shit-rat.

My father had been through a year of hell fighting the social services, and I felt terrible when I became aware of what was happening. When I was younger, I hated my family — sure, lots of kids do — but I really *hated* mine, and I remember during the tough times that I actually wanted to be sent to a foster home. I thought if I had been taken away, things would be so much better. I had fantasies of a Christmas where everyone was happy and grateful for the things they had in life and the people that surrounded them. It seemed like a magical dream.

Now, things were so much better between Dad and me. He truly loved and supported me. There was no way I would let him down again. In hindsight, that McDonald's incident could have ended up a whole lot worse than just getting fired. I could have destroyed his whole effort to keep the house and raise me.

That first night Mom was gone seemed strange. It was different from the times she had gone into rehab — I can't even describe it. Dad and I had our usual ritual watching *Hockey Night in Canada* and eating spaghetti. Life seemed too good to be true — it was uncomfortable. I kept waiting for the next terrible thing to happen.

I even asked Dad if everything was going to be okay. He didn't answer, but his eyes welled up, and he even cried a little. I asked again and he shot me a look like, *don't bug me.*

We never spoke about it again.

Then, for some reason, my father stopped speaking to me. It really bothered me, especially because it wasn't set off by any specific antics, so, after a few weeks while we were watching hockey I stood up and walked over to him in his chair.

I took a deep breath and told him that I was sorry for causing him and Mom so much grief as a kid and that I now knew if I worked hard, I could be successful.

He put his beer down, looked me in the eye and said, "Really, what are you going to do?"

I told him I was going to work really hard to become a firefighter and try to make it in hockey. But he laughed — not a little laugh but a deep belly chuckle.

"Dad," I said, "I'm not joking — I'm going to do my best. I'm going to work really hard at hockey, maybe see if I can play in university, and get an education." He liked what I was saying and started smiling.

Then he began to cry, and said, "I was so worried they were going to take you away from me, you understand?" I nodded and he repeated it louder with his eyes welling up, "Do you understand?"

I said that I did and that I was so sorry for everything and promised to make it up to him. After a few minutes of silence, Dad said, "You end up becoming a firefighter, that's going to be a good day son, a very good day." He wiped his eyes as the Maple Leafs scored on the Canadians and Danny Gallivan screeched out *goal!* The mood lightened and I went into the kitchen.

My dad was right about the hockey dream being a long shot, but I was going to be a firefighter and had said as much. Vancouver Fire Hall Number Two was right down the street from where I used to box, and I had seen the engine flying out on responses on multiple occasions. Then there was a second dream of mine — scoring the winning goal in the Stanley Cup Finals.

Hockey tryouts went well. I made the B Rep team easily and even scored a couple practices with the A team. I stayed late at school doing extra work to get a better mark. My high school was the laughingstock of Vancouver, however, so the teachers really didn't care about my newfound attitude. A few of them still humoured me.

There were several times where I had to consciously stay away from trouble. The group of losers would still come around, throwing me up against the lockers or punching me in the head, but I never reacted, just took the hits and kept my head down.

One day, some of us were walking home and a buddy got challenged to a fight. He said he wanted to go, just needed to take his jacket off, but as soon as he started to pull the sleeves over his arms the other guy started hammering him with punches. My buddies stepped in, and I stepped out — *that* was hard to do. My buddy was an awesome fighter, and once he got his arms free, he totally destroyed the guy with a dozen hard shots to the head. The downside was both my buddy and the other guy got suspensions when a teacher showed up on the way to his car and nabbed them both. Thankfully, I stayed out of it and took off running when the teacher showed up. That was my new life, staying out of trouble at all costs.

I went to some parties around that time, and while I did have a few drinks, I wouldn't smoke any weed. Weed was the latest and greatest thing because it was so easy to get. All my friends were smoking at least a few times a week. I'd still hang with them, but I just wouldn't do it. They would always bug me, asking me if I was chicken, but I had too much to lose and had made a promise to my father. Sure, sometimes there was six of us in a car, with five of my friends lighting up and me abstaining — I got stoned second-hand through pure osmosis, but never ever directly smoked a joint — not once.

Christmas was just around the corner and things were going well especially in hockey. I was scoring lots of goals and throwing the big hits, doing what I did best. There were several opportunities to fight out on the ice, but I backed off each time — I really wanted to stay absolutely and completely out of trouble.

One game, the coach pulled me aside and told me that we were up against a tough team and that he wanted me to set the tone. I told him I would. On my first shift I hammered four guys. One wanted to fight me, but I turned away and went to the bench. The coach came up immediately and asked if I was okay — he was *not* happy that I didn't throw fists.

The coach later accepted that I just wasn't the fighting type and left me alone. But I *was* the fighting type. I just had to control it to uphold my promise to Dad.

All was not calm on the home front. My basement-dwelling brother, who had finished his university degree and was unemployed, hated my father for having my mother removed from the house. He never came upstairs anymore. The high-strung tension ended explosively one day when my brother went crazy and started smashing everything in the house. My sister was home and called my dad in a panic. Dad called his lawyer who told me to call my sister back and tell her to get out of the house immediately. She went outside, taking cover in her car and the emergency police response team showed up, guns drawn. They entered our home, and my sister drove away. My brother completely vanished after that, never coming back to our home.

The house began to feel very depressing again. *How could that be?* I thought. But we had two roof leaks, an abundant colony of mice, and one day I left the door open and someone came in and stole what little possessions we still had, throwing everyone into a funk.

Christmas rolled around, and everyone was depressed. It was so quiet. Although my mom was a drunk, she had been the one who gave us presents; but she was gone, and there were no gifts under the tree that year. No chocolates and mandarin oranges in our stockings. After everything that had happened in the last couple of years — all the terrible fighting, especially on that day — I still missed her terribly that Christmas morning.

Social Services did a check on us and my father told my sister and me that we needed to keep doing what we were doing. My hockey was going well. On average, my grades were in the C range, although I had a B in both Woodshop and Band. All in all, it was the best report card I had ever received. No failures and several nice comments from teachers. Although I was doing better than before, I was really struggling with remembering the lessons. I would make flash cards and go over the questions again and again but then, at the exam, it seemed I had been studying the wrong things the whole time. It was so frustrating because I was trying so hard. Dad couldn't afford a tutor so I would check in with learning assistance for pointers. I had to really work hard just to be average in school but, coming from where my grades used to be, I was overjoyed to get anything higher than a C.

After Christmas, I played a hockey tournament with the Rep B team and did well, prompting a call-up to play in a couple games for the Rep A team, which was awesome! I was comfortable in my skating stride and had a hitting style that no one saw coming. If they wanted to carry the puck, I wanted to hit them. It was so much fun. I was called up to the A team several more times toward the end of the year.

Then hockey was finished, and it was the best season I had ever played. I led the team in goals, assists, and hits, but not penalties. I was in the groove. One game I scored five goals and three assists. It was during an away game against Vancouver Minor in the Forum, where the Vancouver Canucks used to play decades ago. I remember Dad not being in a good mood and on the way home, reminding me of several things I didn't do well. I remember thinking, *Who the hell is he to tell me that? I just scored 5 goals, and he's never played the game*. I listened all the same, because to say what I was thinking would only hurt his feelings.

Football and lacrosse started up where hockey left off. I loved the contact of both sports —they were so fast and physical. I wasn't very good but enjoyed the camaraderie. I played as a tight end. On our team, there was always a rift between defense and offense. The first game of the season, I caught a twenty-yard pass midfield and ran it in for a sixty-yard touchdown — I thought it was the start of an amazing year.

I was wrong. I rarely got the ball thrown to my side and then, in lacrosse, I was on the bottom line. I was fine with it because most of the kids had played their whole lives. For me, it was just fun to play.

Before I knew it, lacrosse and football were over too. It was the end of June and I started working at the cannery again for the summer. It was going to be awkward, however, because Mom still worked there.

I hadn't seen or spoken to my mother in what seemed like a year. I began losing sleep thinking about how I would handle seeing her. I felt totally responsible for her being yanked from the house and taken away from her family. Then there was the time when I hit her, and the guilt was still eating me alive. Harry Rankin had interviewed me several times and I said I wanted to stay with Dad and promised my behaviour would improve. Rankin warned that if I didn't stay out of trouble, I would be removed. I signed the affidavit, and after the court proceedings, my mother was physically removed, kicking and screaming. My life had seemed so different since then but I hadn't even thought much about how this affected my mom. Now, with the cannery job coming up, I was worrying about her. Everyone at the cannery now knew we were related and I debated not going back, but couldn't resist the fifteen-dollar an hour wage, not to mention the potential overtime, double-time and sometimes even triple-time earnings. I decided I would go in for the first day and just test the waters.

The night before my first shift, I didn't get any sleep. I caught the 5:15 am bus and arrived at work by 6:40 — fifty minutes before starting time. The other workers showed up, milling around the lunchroom before starting. My mom walked in at 7:00. She didn't look towards me. The air felt thick, and it was hard to breathe.

It seemed like hours before we went to our stations, me going to the icehouse and my mom heading to the filleting table. The icehouse was -15 degrees Fahrenheit, about fifty-feet long, twenty-feet high and ten-feet wide. An auger ran down the middle of the floor, end-to-end — when it started turning, I started shoveling. Some days, I spent twelve hours in that place.

The first few weeks, the crew worked fourteen-to-sixteen hours a day. There were so many fishing boats coming in, all loaded to the brim. After the first week, I stopped going into the lunchroom in the mornings so I only saw my mom a few times from afar.

The cannery hit a lull, and I had five days off in a row towards the end of July. It was the first time all summer that I got to hang out with my friends. Overall, I didn't mind working. The money I was making was crazy-good and seeing Mom off-and-on wasn't hard — I was used to ignoring her and we never spoke. I honestly think she wanted to come and talk with me, but I never gave her the opportunity. A couple of times we would be walking towards each other and I would either turn around or walk in a different direction.

More than a few people at the cannery told me how nice my mom was, how she was such a good person. I loved my 'sober mom'— she was the greatest lady who'd done so much for me as a kid. I have very fond memories of her tucking me in when she was sober, leaving me a dollar every day for lunch, buying a dozen TV dinners for me to eat for a couple of weeks when she worked late and *then* went over to my grandma's place to give her pills. Sometimes it was after midnight when she arrived home by bus — all this, only to have to get up at 4:30 again the next morning to go back to work. Even as a young kid, I knew she cared about me. She was just owned by the bottle. That part, it seemed, would never change.

I used to tell people that when my mom was removed from the house, it was the best day of my life. Someone once said to me, "If that was your best day, I would hate to hear your worst."

I said, "It was the same day."

I felt so bad for my mom, and my hand in the proceedings. I can't imagine how she felt, being a mother, regardless of a drinking or drug problem, and not being able to see her kids again.

I finished the last few weeks of work without incident. Altogether, I made sixteen-thousand dollars for that summer's work — tons of money for a kid just entering grade eleven. With that heap of money, I bought a car even though I was only fifteen and didn't have a driver's license. I had my dad insure it under his name, that way it could be driven by him to and from the shop as I was getting it fixed up.

The car was a 1974 Pontiac Astre station wagon, a total piece of crap — but two of my buddies had Chevy Vegas — exactly the same vehicle with a different name.

My dad would leave the house for work early, coming home at six in the evening, so every once in awhile, I would sneak out and drive the car around the block. Then I would slip out and drive it to the store. Before I knew it, I was driving it to school every day. I knew that I was supposed to keep my nose clean, but I saw no harm in driving *my* car even though I didn't have a license. At least it was insured, and I was super careful. I know now how foolish it was, but I had confidence, life was going well and as long as I didn't hit anything, it was fine in my mind.

Then one day, driving home, I pulled up to an intersection, and a police car arrived at the same time. He motioned for me to go, and then followed me for a couple of blocks. I was shitting my pants until he turned off. I pulled up to my house, parked, and never drove the car illegally again. I truly thought it was God sending me a warning sign.

I got my learner's license one month later.

School was no longer as terrifying as it had been for me with less of the constant sickening feeling I was used to. I still didn't like school, but aside from being thrown down or shoved around by that gang of losers, attendance was feasible with my home life quiet.

People started to notice my confidence. Girls began to feel comfortable around me and I started to feel the same. I had several girls for friends, and was attracted to them, but didn't have the nerve to ask them out. I didn't do anything beyond just speaking to them.

All the same, the school year started off a little bumpy. One of the usual thugs threw a punch at me when I was opening my locker. I saw it coming and threw back the door, and he hammered his fist into my locker. I turned around and grabbed him, holding down his arms, and yelled right in his face for the whole school to hear, "Enough!"

Then, when I pushed him away, he screamed, "You're a dead man!"

For the first couple of weeks, I was looking over my shoulder. Nothing ever came of it, but that confidence I had evaporated.

Hockey started up again, and I was carded as a Casual A player, meaning I played for both the Rep B and Rep A teams as needed. I got my full driver's license, which opened up a new world for me and my buddies. We used to drive down Hastings after midnight and hang around Davie Street. There was always lots happening there. Vancouver had several 'red-light districts,' like Richards and Gore Streets, the big one being Davie Street. Davie also had restaurants, clubs, and bars, and at the foot of it, a spectacular beach called English Bay.

Vancouver was truly a beautiful city and now that I had a car, my buddies and I would cruise the streets in my Astre. Every weekend and some week-nights we would cruise around and before calling it a night, we'd end up at Bino's Restaurant around three or four in the morning for a burger.

CHAPTER TEN

Sex Changes Everything

I was sixteen. It was a Friday night in November, and I was meeting my buddies Rich, Marco, and Rob at Marco's house. On the way, I decided to drive through the McDonalds to grab a Big Mac. I ordered at the speaker, as usual, but when I pulled up to get my food, the girl at the window said, "Hi Steve." Hearing my name caught me totally off guard.

She was a cute little blond girl named Charlie, in grade ten. I knew her brother, who was widely known as a fantastic hockey goalie. We had never spoken before, although I'd noticed her around the school, and she was a year younger than me. She passed out my food and asked if I would be able to give her a ride home. She was just finishing her shift. I was stunned, and to be honest, didn't really want to, but didn't want to hurt her feelings either.

So I said okay, and minutes later there was Charlie and a waft of perfume climbing into my car. She lived only about a mile from the McDonalds. I was thinking that soon enough I'd drop her off and go meet up with my buddies for our usual drive downtown. She asked me what I was up to that night and I told her about our downtown adventures. As we talked, I noticed how nice she smelled. We drove down Parker Street, and before turning into her lane, she asked if I had time to go for a little drive. I told her I was already late and that I had to go. But she insisted, saying it would only take a few minutes and that she really needed to talk to me. She made it sound serious. I was suddenly interested in what she had to say so we drove on for a while. Then, she told me to drive up Burnaby Mountain.

Burnaby Mountain overlooks the City of Vancouver. It was the place everyone went to make out. We parked and before I knew what was happening, she had her tongue down my throat and her hand in my pants. That was the first time I had been aroused by physical contact with someone — not that it went any further than that— but I was ready to explode. Needless to say, I missed my Friday night adventure, and my buddies were furious because I was their transportation. I wasn't attracted to Charlie. She was cute, but all I wanted was sex at that point.

After that encounter, I took her home. Before getting out of the car, she slid over and kissed me while putting her hand on my crotch and moving it around in a circular motion, then said goodbye and left.

Charlie wanted to meet up on the following Saturday, and I was more than willing. I picked her up and we went to my house. Like earlier, before I knew it, she was on her knees pulling my pants down and I was ready to explode. I was concentrating hard on not blowing up before we actually had sex. When we had all of our clothes off and I was on top of her, she told me to make love to her.

I remember that moment like it was yesterday, for two reasons. One, because it was going to be my first time having sex. And two, because she asked a question that hit me like a bucket of cold water.

"Do you have a condom?"

I said, "What?" and "No, I don't." *I hadn't even thought of that.*

She calmly said, "Well this can't happen then." She started to put her underwear back on. I was so horny — my mind racing, thinking there must be another way — I was frantic. My moment was quickly evaporating.

So I blurted out: "How about Saran Wrap?"

She looked at me like I was a nutbar and said, "You're joking, right?"

I didn't respond because I wasn't joking.

We sat on the couch fully clothed now and watched a movie. Then I took her home.

First thing the next morning, I went out and bought three boxes of condoms. An odd number, but a lot of condoms — mostly so I wouldn't have to go through the embarrassment of buying them again — at least not for a *long* time. I waited in the till lineup with a bag of chips, a can of pop, and a magazine for camouflage. I had the boxes covered by the magazine and chips so the people behind me wouldn't see them.

Then came that dreaded, non-reading beeping sound, and the twenty-year-old cashier smiled, saying, "I'll have to get a price check on these." *Where was God now?* I thought.

I quickly said, "It's okay, I'll just leave them," but she was already broadcasting to the entire drug store that I was buying *Trojan, ribbed and lubricated premium latex condoms.* I'm convinced the bitch did it on purpose, enjoying every second of me shriveling to death in that lineup.

And of course, it took five minutes, so the cashier was trying to make small talk. She had the condoms in one hand and asked, "Any big plans this weekend?" And then she laughed.

I left, telling myself that I would never be able to show my face in that store again. But that didn't matter now. I had a wad of condoms and was ready for action.

At noon that same day, I called Charlie and asked if she wanted to meet. But it was weird, she blew me off saying she had stuff to do. I saw her at school, and we chatted. She was pleasant, but we didn't talk about us getting together, or rather she didn't, so I didn't either. I couldn't stop thinking about actually having sex with her. The weirdest part was, even now, I'm not sure if I liked her but I was definitely obsessed with the idea of sex happening.

I saw her at school one morning and though wanting to get together, when she said hi, I didn't reply and kept walking. I didn't know what was going on with her. In the afternoon between classes, I went to my locker and she was there waiting for me. Charlie said she had to babysit her little brother on Saturday and did I want to come over and be with her. I emphatically said yes.

Saturday came around and I was getting ready to go over to Charlie's when the thought popped into my head that I had never put on a condom before. So I excited myself and opened a package and unraveled the condom and tried to slide it on. But it was crazy slippery, and I was fighting to figure it out. I called one of my buddies up out of the blue, and he explained how to roll it on.

I ended up bringing four condoms that night just in case I ran into trouble and needed a backup or two. Charlie opened the door, and she smelled absolutely amazing. That's one thing I remembered — she *always* smelled amazing — or maybe being so horny, I just imagined it. We sat on the couch watching TV while her little brother ran around, tiring himself out. It seemed forever before Charlie put him to bed. She came into the living room and I was ready to go. She sat beside me. I started groping her. She pushed me away and said to slow down. It was weird. I was so excited to be there and get going, but suddenly she seemed totally uninterested.

I folded my arms and was watching TV for about fifteen minutes. Then she was suddenly straddling and kissing me. Before I knew it, she had my pants off and was on her knees using her hand — and that was that, I took all of thirty seconds, and was done — no sex, just a hand job and a night of watching movies. Charlie was so hard to read and it drove me crazy.

Over the next couple of weeks, the same sort of thing kept happening. Every time I thought we were going to have sex, it ended up being everything but. I was dying with frustration having been so fixated on the idea of making love to Charlie.

My hockey coach took me aside after a game and asked me if everything was okay. He could tell I wasn't concentrating and was worried something was wrong. I told him no, that everything was great. Then he straight up asked me if I had a girlfriend and, when I said yes, he yelled, "Son of a bitch!" Then he booted a water bottle across the dressing room. He told me to dump her and concentrate on hockey. He was furious. As he walked out of the room, he turned to me, said "Dump her!" and walked out.

My buddies were angry with me too and started to plan weekends without me. That part happened fast, their dropping me, but I didn't care. I was a man on a mission. For now, my friends and hockey were just going to have to wait.

Whenever I wasn't playing hockey, I was with Charlie every weekend and often a couple of days during the week. Finally, watching a movie in my empty house, she seduced me in every way I'd been imagining. I remember it vividly. It had seemed so magical — in hindsight, it really hadn't been anything special — but at the time, finally making love to a woman for me was spectacular.

After that, I thought I would be okay, and just slide back into my old life but Charlie had other ideas. She had certain tricks like leaving me naughty notes and calling, saying stuff to deliberately turn me on — and all I wanted to do was bang her brains out. I wasn't in love, I was in lust. I couldn't get enough of it. Every time we got together, we had sex, sometimes two or three times a day. It was all I thought about, from the time I got up in the morning until I went to bed at night, and Charlie knew it.

Christmas rolled around, and it was one of the best. My dad, my sister and I were all getting along. I was having sex almost every day and the hockey season was going well, or so I thought. Aside from school, there was very little stress in my life.

Shortly after Christmas, however, I got cut from the A team because the coach said I had turned into a vegetable, telling me to come back and talk to him when I had my head on straight. Sex was dominating my life to the point where (in hindsight) I think I was addicted. Charlie had given me a bunch of incredible Christmas presents, as well as writing me a note saying she had fallen in love with me, and how important I was to her. Apparently, she wanted to spend the rest of her life with me.

I did a huge gut check: *what the hell was I doing? Was I going to marry this girl one day? Is this the woman of my dreams?* My brain went crazy for the next few weeks, mulling over these questions, and I think Charlie could see that.

One weird thing was that her stepdad just hated me. He never spoke to me, always eyeballing and staring me down whenever he had the chance. I tried to avoid him when I could, getting along with Charlie's older brother and her mother instead. There was also her younger brother, the one she babysat occasionally. He was awesome, so full of life and excitable. But seeing another family laid out in front of me only made me question more, if Charlie were the one to marry, I would have to acquire a home, and then kids. *Was* Charlie the one I wanted to do this with?

I was in shock, being relegated to the B team in hockey. I suddenly felt under a ton of stress. My friends were no longer in my life — everything was just Charlie. Over the next few months, she confided in me more and more about the future she was dreaming of. She had become very controlling and even though we were still having sex every time we got together, she wanted me to quit sports. All we did was watch movies and have sex. We never went out with anyone else.

Then one day, we were at my house drinking and watching movies as usual and Charlie told me her stepdad had sexually molested her twice when she was younger. She told me the details, remembering the events clearly.

I freaked out and yelled at her, "You have to tell someone!" She said she couldn't because she loved her mom, and her mom would protect her stepdad. Then she told me she thought she was addicted to sex, and that scared the absolute hell out of me. In that very moment I realised, sooner or later, I was not going to be the main party favour.

Over the next few days, my head was racing. I was withdrawn when we were together. Charlie noticed, and said she felt sorry for telling me, asking me to forget about it so we could move on. We were still having tons of sex, but I was emotionally numb and, for some reason, felt awful afterward.

She was my first, but she had already told me all about the five guys I knew she had dated — God knows how many there were — and she was only in grade ten. I was now in a very different place than I had been when we first met. Charlie was still inside my thoughts all the time, but not in a good way. Now I wanted some normal interaction with my friends. I wanted to be back in my old, unattached life.

So, I decided to start getting some of it back. A bunch of guys were getting together with beer for the birthday of one of my friends. They were meeting at his house and then going out. I hadn't hung out with any of them for months, so I gave Charlie plenty of notice that I was going to attend. She didn't say anything at the time, but I could tell she was furious. On the day of the party, she called me. She told me that she wanted me so badly, begging me to come over —of course, I would be missing the party. But that part of me, that desperation, was gone. I said no, and she slammed the phone down. I couldn't let her do this to me. I really *wanted* my friends in my life again. But moments before I walked out the door, she called again. I ended up at her house that night instead, having our raunchiest, most adventurous sex yet.

Charlie owned me. I started to realize that over the following weeks. She thought if the sex got raunchier, I would be more engaged. Instead, it started to turn me off. I was losing interest even faster, and she could tell. One weekend, I went to hang out with my buddies and didn't tell her. When she found out, she went ballistic. I walked away, telling her that we were done, finished, kaput. It felt amazing saying that, like a weight was lifted.

That showdown gave me some added perspective on where I was headed in life. I couldn't marry this girl — she was clearly not "the one." It would be a disaster. Plus, I didn't even want to think about a long-term relationship right then. I was in freaking high school and there she was wanting me to think about married life. All I wanted was to graduate and just have fun with my friends.

Sure enough, the following Monday, Charlie was back at my locker, whispering sexy stuff in my ear — and before I knew it, I was back, and we were having more sex than ever. I was so weak and so confused — she had power over me that I couldn't explain.

It was now well into February, and we were fighting a lot. Charlie could be so nasty, so hurtful, but it was always fixed with sex. Our entire relationship now revolved around that one physical act. We got into a big fight when I decided to meet up with one of my buddies again. In retaliation for me simply being social, she went to my house and tore my room apart. When I got home and discovered the damage, I called her and told her I was done — for real this time—and hung up on her.

She called back immediately. Her first words were raunchy sex talk. I told her again, adamantly, that I was done, and hung up.

The phone rang again, and again, for over an hour. I took it off the hook. Then she physically came to my house to tell me she couldn't live without me. I told her to get over it, we were done. I was trying hard to stay strong and keep my foot down though I really wanted more raunchy sex and she knew it. I was weak and Charlie preyed on it.

Time flew by and we didn't speak for days. It felt good. My buddies were slowly warming up to me again and I realized it would take work to rebuild those friendships. I was focusing on not letting them down again. But the phone started ringing again. Charlie was becoming neurotic. She was waiting at my locker every day and when I didn't show up, she left post-it notes all over the locker door. Notes even turned up in the mailbox at my house.

Charlie ambushed me one day after school. She started crying, and because other students were around, I took her down a side street. She said she wanted to try being together again and would do whatever I wanted.

Hanging with my friends? No problem. She said she understood and would do whatever she could to make it work. She said she loved me.

But even as she was talking and making promises, I knew it would only be temporary. As long as we were together, she could control me with sex. I said that I was sorry, but I couldn't get back together with her, and walked away. She ran up and grabbed me, then said she would kill herself. Pulling away from her, I walked home.

I got a call that night from her older brother. He didn't know that we had broken up but told me Charlie was in the hospital. She had slashed both her wrists.

I was in shock. I felt like shit. I hung up the phone, sat at my kitchen table and just stared at the fridge. I couldn't *not* go see her — I felt completely responsible. They had Charlie hopped up on meds, and she seemed peaceful and nice. I felt awful, certain that I had caused this incident. She asked me to pick her up some magazines and Pepsi. I did, and then she asked if I would come again tomorrow.

Before I knew it, I was at her house every single day until she was able to go back to school. Charlie said she knew she had issues and was going to work hard on them. She was going to see a counsellor to become a better person. She claimed to understand that while we were no longer together, she thought we could still be friends. I agreed. Charlie asked if I could help her become stronger. I sincerely wanted to be supportive.

As if I had blinked, we were going out again and having sex two or three times a day. I was under a spell again, stuck in a loop. Time started to blur. I wasn't really there during the sex, during any intimacy — it was just a physical motion, followed by laying around listening to her say how much she loved me. Another month passed and hockey ended. I was a total zombie with the life sucked from me. I hated this relationship, and I hated the animosity of her stepfather and the terrible knowledge of what he'd done to her. I felt so trapped. Our sex had become more and more aggressive. The condom ripped on several occasions. Charlie didn't seem to worry about it, so neither did I.

The relationship should have been at a point where I could be comfortable doing what I wanted, that she would be okay with my sports schedule and happy with whatever I decided was best for myself, but she wasn't. It was exactly the same as before.

After a few more weeks in the zombie-state, I finally called it. I literally couldn't do it anymore. I told her that I wasn't sleeping, I was stressed out, and didn't want to think about marriage. We were done for good this time. It felt like she had been waiting for this to happen and was ready this time. She was hysterical, threatening to kill us both. I begged her to understand that there was no way to work it out — I just couldn't be with someone I didn't love. I still cared for her, I explained, but wanted her to be happy with someone else. I walked out.

A week passed, and I barely slept. I was terrified — I'm not really sure of what — but the phone call that I had been dreading never came.

Three weeks later, she was waiting in almost the exact same spot she had the last time we broke up but this time she wasn't sobbing or crying. She looked furious. I walked over and said, "Hey."

She exploded. "I'm fucking pregnant, you asshole!"

It felt like someone had just ripped the heart out of my chest. I was in total shock, stumbling away as she yelled, "How are we going to do this? You're going to have to support me!"

I walked the eleven blocks from the school to my home like a dead man. *What the fuck had just happened?* It was the end of May and I had a football practice that night but didn't go. The coach was furious, and I got benched that weekend. It was a smart move on his part, as I would have been completely useless, just riding the bench. Still, we lost the game and the coach took it out on me. He ranted to the whole team about commitment, even using my name as an example — but I didn't care. I had a far bigger problem on my mind.

The next day was Sunday, and Charlie called and asked to meet. She was sorry for yelling and that she had just been stressing out. I met up with her at the White Spot for coffee. We talked. She said she loved me and was adamant to try and make it work for the baby's sake.

I felt like throwing up. My life, my future was changing forever. I didn't want to talk about it, didn't even want to think about it. I asked her to give me some time to process everything.

I didn't speak to anyone for a week. Charlie phoned multiple times but I didn't pick up, until one day. I was honest, telling her again I didn't love her, and that wouldn't change even with us having a kid. I told her I would support her and the baby. I expected to make between twelve and fifteen thousand dollars that summer and she could have it. I also said I would get a job immediately after graduation and give her whatever she needed for support. She screamed that she didn't want my fucking money and slammed the phone down.

I stayed away from my friends. I was a walking disaster. Several teachers asked me if I was okay, so apparently, it showed. I was on track to graduate with a C+ average, but still had to do final exams. I just could not wrap my head around the idea of being a father.

I had many questions and saw Charlie a few times over the next several weeks. She didn't look any different for someone who was (supposedly) pregnant. I wondered how long it took to carry a baby. I thought about pregnancy in terms of a year so when did a woman start getting bigger? I had no idea, so to help me understand, I asked my English teacher, Ms. Grenier.

Ms. Grenier, or "Ms. G," as we called her, looked puzzled when I asked about a woman carrying a baby. Right away, she asked if I was okay. She told me to stay after class and when we sat down, I broke down and cried for fifteen minutes. She was such an amazing teacher and I felt bad — like I was rotten inside. It was the first time I had talked about it with anyone. She came over and gave me a hug. I told her everything, and then *she* started crying.

When we both stopped crying, she asked me if Charlie looked any different. I said that, honestly, I didn't notice anything. She called in a counsellor, brought them up to speed on the situation. They asked me to come in that Friday after school. I asked Ms. G if she was going to be there and she said yes.

That Friday, I went to Ms. G's classroom. She and the counsellor were both there waiting for me and said they had been doing some research. Ms. G said gently, "Steve, I'm worried that Charlie may be playing with your mind — she may not *really* be pregnant."

My heart stopped. Charlie was so manipulative and calculating — that was exactly the sort of thing she would do, I realized. I felt like a kid who had just walked through the gates of Disneyland — but the thought of this as a possibility also infuriated me. Ms. G was so kind, saying that I could come and sit with her anytime, but to definitely return and let her know what was happening.

I went straight home and called a best friend of Charlie's, someone I also considered to be my friend. She told me that Charlie said she was going to destroy me but didn't know anything about her being pregnant. That was weird. How could Charlie's best friend not know? I asked her to call a friend of mine, who in turn called Charlie's brother directly. He said, point-blank, that she wasn't pregnant. Apparently, he burst out laughing — his last girlfriend had done exactly the same thing to him when they broke up.

When the news made it back to me, I collapsed. I didn't cry, just lay on the floor for hours totally relieved. I'd been reborn and a whole new life was ahead.

I was back with my buddies again, heading downtown every weekend to Davie Street, cruising around Stanley Park, and winding up at the Fresco Inn or Bino's in the early morning. I was also asked to play for a team in the Metropolitan League — it was like Junior B and was intimidating and exciting. Overall hockey was going great.

The weeks leading up to graduation were so much fun, filled with tons of parties. We decided to all rent white tuxedos with tails for the graduation ceremony, so we would stand out from the pack. It was held in the Hyatt Hotel in downtown Vancouver. To get an idea of the scene, hotel security stopped several of the school girls from going in, assuming they were prostitutes, which we all thought was hilarious — all of us being from a very low-income area and, the *one night* we all get dressed up, no one believes us.

My parents were one of a few that weren't there. For some reason my dad didn't come. I still have no idea why, but I'm sure there was a good reason, and it didn't really bother me. After the ceremony, we all went to the Commodore for dancing and then the Blue Horizon on Robson Street to our rooms. It was one was of the best nights of my life — so much fun, and everybody was happy.

The ceremony was on Saturday. I got home late Sunday night and passed out. I slept until late afternoon the next day, stumbled to the bathroom to pee, then went back to bed, waking up on Tuesday at 9:00 in the morning. I never saw Monday.

Graduation was mainly the big build-up weeks ahead, and then in one night it was done. My question was, *What now?* I was going back to the fish cannery for the summer but had zero plans after that. I thought I would work at the fish plant for a year or so, stockpiling enough cash to move out and realize the dream of moving to the downtown core and living a life of freedom —my own place with my own rules. That was what I envisioned.

Grad was amazing to me and I felt on top of the world. My father had no idea what had happened with my 'Charlie experience' over the past year but he was proud of me when I received my grad certificate with an honour roll seal — that was the icing on the cake.

Then the fishing season started, and I worked sixteen hours a day, as many hours as they would give me. I quit football because the coach was terrible, nasty, and didn't like me. I didn't play another season of lacrosse either, just worked my ass off. I never saw or heard from Charlie until we crossed paths one day in a bar at the Lougheed Hotel. I was a little unnerved seeing her, but because my good friends were with me, I overcame that feeling almost immediately.

After Charlie, I was terrified of women for some time. I went on several dates with fantastic girls, but didn't want to have sex, abhorring physical contact in every way. One of my buddies had been going out with his girlfriend for a long time and her best friend really liked me. She was beautiful, funny, and had a perfect body. One evening, we went to a play and then up Seymour Mountain to have a few beers. We went for a walk and then started kissing. She slid her hand down my pants, and I was totally turned on until she pulled me over to the side of the tree line, took off her top and pants and started ripping my clothes off.

It was like someone threw a bucket of cold water on me. I stopped her, and she was so embarrassed. All the way home I explained it wasn't her, it was me, but she didn't believe it. We never went on another date. I was scared. I was damaged goods when it came to women. In fact, after Charlie, I didn't have sex with anyone — until I met Helen that is.

Grade twelve was one of the toughest years of my life. I made the freaking honour roll! Okay, I *did* have a double block in Mechanics, but I also got B's in English and Socials, which were the best grades I ever received. I made the top A team in hockey. Our house went up for sale as soon as I graduated, and I was excited to get out on my own and move downtown to a condo. I felt ready to experience the single life of Vancouver.

CHAPTER ELEVEN

It's a Wonderful Life

Grade Twelve was so behind me: those thugs were gone, so I was no longer looking over my shoulder. That Christmas went far better than the year before. Life was as good as it had ever been, and even my father seemed quite happy. I was thinking of possibly working at the fish company full-time and going to school part-time to take firefighter related courses.

But those thoughts changed after I started working at the cannery on the late night shift. I was working alongside a guy who told me a story of needing some cash one day. Wearing one of his skiing balaclavas and carrying his dad's shotgun, he held up a corner store. As I listened to him, I was reminded of the guys I grew up with. It was the way he spoke about it with such pride, like he was defining how cool he was. I started to analyze everyone I was working with and realized they were all very similar to my old friends. I realized I needed another job. But I wanted to work at a job I enjoyed. I had been making good money and thought that maybe I could go travelling for a bit, then go back for post-secondary school for something I liked.

I was aware that having struggled through high school with my apparent learning disability, I would need to be careful of what sort of schooling I chose. I felt lazy when it came to studying. Those two problems would make post-secondary school very, very difficult unless I kept them in mind and worked through them.

I had two things to think over. One was my future career.

Second, I wanted to speak to my Mom.

I had avoided her for almost three years now and wanted to rebuild our relationship. While we both worked together at the cannery, I never ate in the lunchroom because that's where she ate. Accordingly, I decided I would ease into a reunion by simply eating in the same room again.

We hadn't spoken in years but a couple days into eating in the lunchroom together, she turned and smiled at me, and I waved back.

The next day she brought me a bag lunch and I thanked her. I laughed. It was a peanut-butter and jam sandwich, a cookie, and chocolate milk. Then Mom brought my lunch every day for the rest of my time there.

Mom told me her car was in the shop, so I drove her home. We never spoke about the elephant in room, just talked as if nothing had ever happened. That elephant would not have solved our past so we both pretended it never happened. It was good to have my mother back in my life, despite its awkwardness.

Aside from working with the robber, it turned out to be a great summer. Including all of my overtime, I ended up making over $20,000. By the end of August, I was picking up Mom and dropping her off for every shift. We were friends again. She still drank every night but I didn't have to watch it. I had always dreamed about getting to be with *just* the sober version of my mom and now my wish had been granted.

One day on a drive home I said, "Mom, that day I shoved you …" She stopped me and said, "Those were dark days Steven. I am so proud of you and how good of a person you turned out to be. I never want to talk about those days. There is no need. We have so much to do in the future, I am glad we have a relationship again."

With all of the shit my family had been through that was one of the fondest moments I have ever had with my mother, and to this day, I am so glad something positive came out of our family troubles.

I planned to stay at home with Dad until the house sold but was able to ride on the coattails of some friends who were taking a trip to Europe. I spent two and a half months traveling around the former Yugoslavia, France, and Germany. It was amazing and opened my mind to more travel.

When I came home, I decided to try and get into the *Aircraft Structures* program at the British Columbia Institute of Technology. I sent in an application but was denied due to my poor grade point average for grade ten, eleven and twelve, and lack of calculus and physics. The program, however, was going through some restructuring and as luck would have it, they didn't have enough students for their new course *Aircraft Structures Pre-Apprentice* program. So even without the mandatory courses and grades I was accepted, and was to start in January, only a couple of months away.

I was instructed to report to the Vancouver International Campus. Apparently, Air Canada and nearly every other airline was laying people off by the dozens. The industry looked grim, and so few people had applied for the course that I made it in by default.

I had a Yamaha Enduro 175 motorcycle and rode it every day on the one-hour commute to the airport campus. The course was extremely difficult with tons of calculations and formulas, which explained why they asked me all those physics-questions in the interview.

The weeks flew by, but I hated *every second* of that program. It was far, far worse than high school. The problem was the mathematics. They were way over my head. There was clearly a reason why they did pre-testing and had extensive interviews before selecting students. In the first month my father noticed that I was bummed out. He sat me down and told me that he knew it was hard, but that I was going to have to stick it out and finish. Damn, I loved my dad — he did so much for me over the years and though I really wanted to quit, I didn't want to disappoint him. Of course, my father was right. He was so smart, boiling things down to common sense. I realized if I struggled through to complete and pass the course (I would be at the absolute bottom of the class when it came to marks) I could use it as a trade to apply to a fire department.

So, for a *whole year*, I rode my Yamaha to the BCIT Campus at Vancouver Airport and dragged my sorry ass into the classroom and did my best. It was a hard year, with no going out, no time to do anything else but school. But, in the end, I passed the class and was given a certificate to go out into the world and try to find a structural airframe job. Sure enough, there were a few positions up north, but nothing with any of the big airlines that gave all the free flights and other perks.

After a couple of months with no luck finding work, I realised that all that money I had made last summer was almost gone. Over the next few weeks, waves of anxiety started to hit me; I felt lost and unsure of my future.

Then, like it was meant to happen, for the first time in years, Vancouver Fire Department posted for two new firefighter positions. I scrambled to figure out how to put together a resume, then I sent in my application. The clouds had broken, and it felt wonderful.

An article in the Vancouver Sun printed that it was the largest response the fire department had ever had, with over five-thousand applicants for the two jobs. The numbers didn't bother me. For some reason, I just *knew* that I was going to get one of those jobs.

I received a letter a few weeks later inviting me to physical testing, where I would participate along with twelve-hundred other applicants to go to the next round. I was running every single day, doing weight training, and I felt confident I would do well — and I did.

Sure enough, a few weeks later, along with three hundred and ninety-seven other candidates, I was invited to take the written testing portion up at Simon Fraser University. That part terrified me. I wasn't the brightest but had been told fire departments didn't necessarily look for the highest scores on the written test alone, so I was hopeful. The exam was held in an enormous auditorium. I checked in by giving my driver's license at the door. It was intimidating with four hundred finely tuned athletes, vying for literally *two* jobs. The exam was not that bad, except that it had several physics questions and, of course, I struggled on that section.

I handed in my test and walked out feeling good — the only thing left to do was wait until I got the call for the interview. But the call never came. They took sixty candidates to the interview stage, and I wasn't one of them. I was devastated. I knew the odds had been against me and it was only my first attempt getting a firefighting position, but I was still crushed. I had no job and was running out of money fast. The next few months dragged on and on. I started drinking, staying out with my buddies until late, and sleeping in until the afternoon. My father always kept a good tab on me, and he could see I was depressed about where I was in life. The court order from Social Services was in full swing, with the house up for sale and my mother cleared from paying child support — she never had to pay, which was great because she didn't have enough for herself, and because my father wouldn't accept any from her.

Our house took almost two years to sell in one of the worst housing markets in history. My father was terrified to live on his own.

It was only a matter of time before Dad and I would be out searching for a new place to live. Again, my dream to land a job as a firefighter, and move into an apartment in downtown Vancouver and just live on my own and travel, seemed distant.

Have you ever seen that movie, *It's A Wonderful Life*? I felt like George Bailey. I remember the first time I watched that movie — I swear, when George is running around trying to get a suitcase—it brought me back to that part of my life. The dream of getting away from my family, living life on my own, seemed so magical to me. But when my dad went to look for places to live, he became withdrawn and depressed and said he was not looking forward to living alone. When he went looking for a new place, he said he just couldn't imagine living in it by himself — so I suggested we move in together. We found a townhouse and worked it so he put down the thirty-two thousand dollars for the deposit and in turn, I would make the mortgage payments. When we sold it, he and I would split the return fifty-fifty. I liked the idea, and I honestly had no problem putting my single life on hold for a bit. Dad was important to me. I loved him. I was happy to do it.

Dad came into my room one Sunday morning and told me to put something nice on, because we were going to church. I said no thanks, and he replied, "Not an option. Be in the car in fifteen minutes." I was as agnostic as they come, but sure enough, I was putting on nice clothes — mainly because girls would be there.

One of the big downsides to going to church is that the all the kids there grew up together. They had dinners together, travelled together, held weekly barbeques, and attended church every Sunday. They were like a family, and I was some shithead from the hood. They didn't want an outsider coming into their group.

But that didn't matter to my father. We piled into his truck and drove down Hastings to the East Vancouver Orthodox Church. Those first few minutes of arriving at the church was always intimidating, but Vanessa saw me and called me over to sit with her and Yvonne. They were super friendly, always laughing. The funny thing was, those girls were very beautiful, but I just wasn't attracted to them in that way. In fact, in a lot of ways I was still turned off about dating. I wasn't in the market for another relationship. A buddy of mine was trying to get me out to sleep with some girl, any girl, to 'get my mojo back' — but not only did I not have that kind of confidence, I would be self-conscious about hurting her feelings.

Before I left that Sunday Vanessa asked if I wanted to join their dance group, and, of course, I declined. I couldn't dance if my life depended on it. But then my dad found out about that offer and said I *was* doing it — and, before I knew it, I was dancing with the Serbian Orthodox Kolo Group twice a week. We went to festivals, and it turned out to be fun. I also managed to land a full-time job at a stationery warehouse where a buddy of mine already worked. In the meantime, I waited for the next fire department to hire.

A friend, Maya, had her little sister in that same Kolo group. She was always trying to get us in the same room, going out and doing things together. Her sister's name was Melanie, and she was a great girl. We certainly got along, but there was zero romantic chemistry — that, or I was broken and didn't like girls anymore. Charlie had left a scar on me that I wasn't sure I would ever get over. She had faked a pregnancy and had nearly killed herself over our relationship. I never wanted to go through that again.

Melanie and I went out several times and, while it was fun, nothing happened between us. We both just accepted that we would remain friends.

One day, Yvonne suggested that I should take her and her friend Helen skiing after she'd overheard that I used to ski race. I really liked Yvonne, not in a romantic way. And her friend Helen was one of the most beautiful girls I had, and have, ever seen. Yet she seemed stuck up, so I wasn't really excited about her joining us.

Yvonne insisted I should take them up to Cypress Mountain. I thought they would go off and hang together and I would bring some cheese and wine and try and make it into a fun event. Yvonne gave me their addresses. I agreed to pick her up first, *then* go get Helen — I didn't want to be in the car alone with Helen, mainly because although we had held hands during that dance group, we had never spoken a word to each other before or after that. I went out and bought cheese, crackers, and wine, and tried to look forward to Saturday.

Friday night I got a call from Yvonne saying that she couldn't go anymore but that Helen was still interested. To put it lightly, I was not impressed.

I wanted to cancel but I didn't even have Helen's phone number, just her address, so the only way I could shutter the whole thing would be to physically drive to her house, and it was almost 10:00 PM. No cancellation could happen now.

I got up early in the morning and drove to her house. She was waiting outside and hopped in the car. It was the most awkward ride to the ski mountain I had ever taken. We said maybe five words to each other. I'm not sure what Helen was planning, but she didn't even have money to buy a ski ticket, so I had to buy hers, and then it turns out that she didn't know how to ski.

It was an interesting start to a date. Since she couldn't ski, I had to stay right beside her, even guiding her down parts of the runs. There was lots of physical contact and I started to feel very comfortable around her. After a dozen chair lifts up, we were talking up a storm. I had totally misread her. She wasn't stuck up. She was just very shy. How could a girl that beautiful be that shy? It intrigued me. She was charming and kind.

We had a great day, finishing it off with sparkling wine, cheese, and crackers. I'm not sure how she felt about the day but for the first time since Charlie, I wanted to see this girl again. I was twenty and she was in Grade Twelve, a two-and-a-half-year age gap, and I wasn't sure if that was too much, or what people would say. All these reasons why I shouldn't ask her out were racing through my head, but all the way back to her house, I kept thinking about a way to ask her out again, or what would happen if she said no. If she declined me, I would never be able to show my face at that church again. The whole drive back I couldn't work up the nerve, and before I knew it, we were at her house. She thanked me for a nice day and started to get out of the car.

My heart was racing and I quickly blurted out, just as she was about to close the door: "I'm not sure if you'd ever want to do that again, but, if you do, I wouldn't mind seeing you again!"

She smiled, turned and said, "434-0530."

And I'll never, ever forget those numbers!

Weeks passed before I got the nerve to call, and she seemed happy to hear from me. I asked her out, and she said she would love to. She hadn't even graduated from high school, so she made it *very* clear when and where I was to pick her up and drop her off because her parents were very strict.

On our second date, we went for a walk around Stanley Park at night. We talked and laughed and the whole time my heart was racing. Every time we got together after that my heart would start racing. We never kissed or did anything, just went out for dinner, or to plays, finishing every night with a walk around Stanley Park. I quickly fell head over heels for this girl but was absolutely terrified to make a move. I didn't want to ruin anything.

Helen graduated from high school and was taking part in *Miss Teen Vancouver* as a runner-up. I was taking fire sciences courses and dating one of the most beautiful women in Vancouver. I couldn't get the thoughts of becoming a firefighter, marrying Helen, having kids, and living happily ever after out of my mind. I was so in love with her. By now we were kissing, but we had not had any serious physical contact.

I had no confidence to make a move. I had lots of experience when it came to having sex, but no experience on how to make it happen.

To complicate things, Helen's sister Maryanne was a massive influence on her. She took Helen to parties every Saturday night. They went to parties in East Vancouver, Burnaby or on the North Shore – hotspots for pot and cocaine. There was a lot of peer pressure. I knew how I felt about drugs but was worried about Helen because of her sister and the fact that the crowd she hung around with was rough. Plus, Helen was playing volleyball with this one guy I knew she liked, so after a few months I decided I was going to see where we were in our relationship.

There was no doubt in my mind we were going out. I just wanted to confirm it and maybe it would boost my confidence enough to take our relationship to the next level. I was so madly in love with her. I felt safe and she was kind.

I bought pink champagne, twelve pink balloons, pink cream cheese, and even wore pink underwear. One late Friday night, I took Helen to Hallelujah Point in Stanley Park. I put down a blanket where we could sit and look at the city lights. I gave her the balloons, opened the picnic basket, took off my clothes down to my pink underwear, and proposed that we go steady. It had been six months since our first date, and I was fairly sure where we were at but wanted to seal the deal so we could start thinking about the future. She was so happy that I had created all this atmosphere. She was smiling and laughing, holding her sparkling wine. She kept saying how nice it was that I did all of this. I told her I wanted it to be special, and that I was in love with her. I wanted to start thinking about our future and wanted to confirm that we were on exactly the same page.

"We *are* going out, right?"

Helen held her wine and just stared out into the city lights… she never said anything… she started to, then stopped.

I was stunned. Apparently, I had it all wrong, and we weren't going out. She enjoyed my company, but clearly she also liked another guy and was unsure. I was fucking devastated. I packed everything up and dropped her off. She said sorry as she got out of the car and told me she really did like me before closing the door.

I drove the long drive back to my house and stared at the ceiling for what seemed like days. Helen and I stopped calling each other, and I stopped going to the Kolo dance group.

The depressing times of my life seemed to come after some climactic event, and always in waves. I was not sure if that was normal for everyone, but that was my experience.

I was stuck in that rut of feeling down for about three weeks before I looked at what I still had in my life: a father who I really loved, a mother who had returned to my life, and a warehouse job.

I dusted myself off and tried to focus on getting in shape and writing firefighter exams. I started playing hockey again in the Metropolitan Hockey League. But it was 'goon hockey,' with all the other players about the caliber of Junior B, the teams made up of a bunch of washed-up players who never made it to the show. There were two Burnaby teams in the league; as well as one team for Squamish; one for Everett, Washington; and then a Valley team. I was one of the smallest players when it came to weight but skated around hitting everyone I could — for that I was liked.

Aside from the warehouse job, things were going well. I was still dreaming about moving out into my own pad and living the single life in Downtown Vancouver. My father, however, was starting to feel depressed about how his life had turned out. He couldn't see how unhappy he'd been before when my mother was living with us and they were both drunk most of the time. In the meantime, as a good distraction, I was hanging out with friends.

One Friday night, I went over to my friends Maya and Alan's house and Helen's older sister was there, the one who loved parties. She immediately laid into me, calling me an asshole for how I dumped her sister. I had no idea what she was talking about. When I asked Helen if we were going out and she couldn't answer the question, I thought that was an answer in and of itself. But Maryanne said that Helen really liked me and was so upset that I never called her again. I didn't believe her. I thought she was just trying to make me look bad. So I said if Helen really felt that way, she should call me and I would one-hundred percent apologize to her. Maryanne laughed at me and didn't answer.

How does this happen? I would get comfortable then suddenly blindsided by some situation I read completely wrong. It had been months since that date at Stanley Park where I felt I had completely embarrassed myself, and what Maryanne said to me was killing me — so I decided to call Helen after months of no contact.

If you know me personally, you know that I'm a talker, especially when I'm nervous. So, when I called Helen, I talked for ten minutes straight without her getting a word in. I told her how I felt about that night, that I had thought we were an item, that I was totally into her and, when she couldn't answer me, I had felt so embarrassed.

When I died out and Helen spoke, she said at the time she had just graduated from high school and was looking forward to having some freedom and fun and just wasn't sure if she wanted to be in a relationship. She admitted she had been seeing someone else, but that she had really enjoyed our relationship and that night in Stanley Park had been one of the most romantic things anyone had ever done for her. I apologized for putting pressure on her and told her I wasn't very good at dating. We both had a laugh, and that broke any remaining tension. Helen said that, if I was okay with restarting, she would still like to go out. I said that I was and that I would have no expectations about our relationship, so we made a date for the upcoming weekend.

It was one of the most fun, relaxing dates I have ever had. It felt so natural and I was still very comfortable with Helen. We went to a play, ending the night with a walk around Stanley Park, and then when I dropped her off, we both started to lean towards each other to kiss, when I said "I am so sorry I can't".

At that very moment I realized I was still terrified of dating, but at the same time I had that butterfly feeling in my stomach. I blew the reconciliation kissing part, but Helen did not seem bothered by it at all.

I floated all the way home. Emotionally, I was right back to where I was months ago when I was seeing her — head over heels in love.

The weeks went on. Helen started coming out to my hockey games. I was working away at that warehouse job, and for the most part, my life was back on track again. I was in great shape and had a girl in my life that I was crazy about. I just loved being with her.

A while later, we were relaxing in the car at Stanley Park, and I just couldn't control myself. My hands started to make their way around Helen's body, a little more than ever before — but after a bit, she stopped me. She didn't say no, she just said, "Not here."

In the next few weeks, we became very intimate.

"Okay", I said, "can I assume we're actually going out now?"

Helen smiled and said, "I sure hope so."

Building a relationship takes commitment. It takes patience, love, and respect. Sometimes there are arguments, maybe even not talking for a few days. Incredible make-up sex.

Even through some of the craziness, even though I didn't have the foundation in my childhood to help me place the building blocks with Helen, this relationship was different and I knew in my heart that this could be forever.

Fire departments were not hiring in the first year of our relationship, so I decided to try and move up in the warehouse company. They had thirty-two sales representatives and I thought it could be a good position until I landed a firefighter job. I applied, went through some courses, and before I knew it, I was working as a sales rep and was suddenly making very good money. The position came naturally to me — I was very comfortable talking to people.

The downside of the position was that all the other sales reps ate lunch together in the local show lounges and drank on the job, then ended up in the bar every night after work. I took part in the madness for about a year until Helen said she had had enough. She said I was drinking every day and was barely around during the week. Unless I was going to change, she was done. Our relationship would be over.

I was stunned. I didn't see that coming. When I looked back on how I had been acting, she was totally right. I was going to the bar every night after work, not even scheduling calls for Friday afternoon, meaning I would be in the bar from noon until 6:00 pm. Then I would go to meet Helen, usually fairly drunk around the time I picked her up, and yes, I had to leave my car multiple times because I was too intoxicated, and Helen always came and picked me up. She became very tired of my new lifestyle, and rightfully so.

I was embarrassed by who I was as a sales rep, but happy with how I ultimately handled it once Helen laid down the law. I really tried to be good and stay away from the bars but, sure enough, I ended up getting razzed by my superiors and co-workers. I started to sneak a bar visit in every once and a while and, before I knew it, I was right back to doing it every day again. Helen saw what was happening and told me to seriously change, or she was gone.

I was terrified, so much so that the next day I walked into my manager's office and quit. He was stunned. I was making huge money, was "rookie salesman of the year" just the year before. He asked why and what was I going to do? I told him that I had a drinking problem, and I had no idea what I was going to do, but I just needed to quit.

A buddy of mine worked at Stong's Groceries and mentioned to me that they were hiring baggers. I applied and was stocking shelves and bagging groceries at Stong's Grocery within the week. I decided to get my first aid ticket, take some more fire department courses, and wait for the opportunity to apply again.

The thing about my journey as a salesperson was how weak I was. Without Helen giving me notice and a wake-up call, I could have easily become "that guy". Hanging out with sales guys who were extremely successful financially, wearing a suit every day, and driving a brand-new sports car, I was also successful (or so I believed), with a ton of confidence. When I look back to that time, thankfully Helen was in my life to get me back on track.

Nanaimo Fire Department was hiring. I applied, did the physical and received a letter for an interview. Before I knew it, I was sitting in Nanaimo city hall being interviewed by five people from human resources and the fire department. I felt it went really well and two weeks later, I received a letter stating I was listed with nine others for a new fire hall opening in the next twelve months. There was a notation on my letter suggesting I work at getting more medical experience.

Fast forward six months. I was still bagging groceries and stocking shelves and had no word from Nanaimo Fire on a starting date. Helen and I were doing great, and I had managed to become a casual drinker again, not relying on the stuff. My boss at the grocers was a total asshole, always riding everyone, two-faced — needless to say, we didn't get along at all. I was taking an auto extrication course and saw a posting for a full-time ski patroller and thought that would be a great experience. I was a good skier, and sure as hell didn't want to work in a grocery store for the rest of my life. The problem was that the ski patroller job paid eleven bucks an hour, and I was bagging groceries for twenty-one bucks an hour — it was a harsh difference financially, but the medical experience would be great.

I made the decision to quit as it would be fantastic medical experience and would potentially change my course in life, hopefully for the better. I was working the floor during a night shift with a friend named Rob, and I told him I was going to quit. Funny thing was, Rob said the manager was going to try and talk me into staying, so we decided that I should not show up for work the next day and call in to quit over the phone the next day as the next two-week schedule was just about to be completed. I didn't care about giving this guy two weeks' notice — he was such an asshole — it was my small opportunity to hit back. I had seven applications out with other local fire departments, was in the best shape of my life, and with the Nanaimo letter I was hopeful for the future — my manager could eat it.

Rob and I finished waxing the floors and locked up, closing the store around midnight. I drove home, excited to execute my plan the next day.

I got up late the next morning and tried calling into the store, but the line was busy. I tried multiple times, but it was still held up, which was odd. So I called the head office, and the woman who picked up told me the store

I worked in was robbed last night, totally cleaned out, and that there was suspicion that it was an inside job.

The phone dropped from my hand in shock. The store was robbed *the same day* I didn't show up for work, and they thought it was an inside job. I drove my sorry ass down to the store. There were cops everywhere. The manager asked me where the hell I had been, and I told him I had a family issue. He just glared. The police interviewed everyone, even people who hadn't worked at all in the last few days. They interviewed everyone—everyone but me.

I was convinced that I was under surveillance, so I stayed at the grocery store for several more months just so it didn't look like I was part of the break-in. My fear was they would somehow find my childhood record and I would be guilty just because of my regrettable past. By the time I was ready to quit, the ski patrol job was long gone but the local mountains got absolutely no snow that season, so there wouldn't have been work anyway. After a couple of months I thought I would throw my application in just in case. They said they had enough staff for ski patrollers, but that they would still hold onto it.

I was just finishing up at Stong's when the Grouse Mountain Ski Patrol called me and said they had a supervisor's position open. Sure enough, I was shortly working with them, setting up ropes for the runs, and was second in charge for avalanche blasting. That year, everyone was new except for two guys, so they had me as one their supervisors. I was making barely over half of what I was at the grocery store but was finally learning some hands-on medical and leadership skills.

The snow came all at once— seventeen feet of the white stuff in seventeen days, a new record for the area — and the ski season went from dead to super busy. We alternated working one week of days and one week of afternoons. It was incredible fun and I got tons of medical experience. The mountain ran at capacity on weekends and nights whenever there was a good snow. We had broken legs, broken arms, dislocated shoulders, and concussions daily — but this was also the year we had four missing persons lost for longer than a day. One poor old German guy spent five days out there, lost on the mountain, but survived the cold temperatures by sleeping in a tree well.

I had one of the few near fatalities of the year in my first week. It was unnerving for me. I'd never done CPR before, but I was the first patroller on scene by about ten minutes. We did CPR for about forty-five minutes while we prepared him and got him back to the gondola. By that time the paramedics had come up the mountain. They used their AED (automated external defibrillator) and he came back — they got a pulse. I remember that being the biggest thing — he left alive. *That* was a great feeling, but I was shell-shocked immediately after.

I walked around looking for my patrol backpack. I couldn't find it, even asking another patroller if he'd seen it. He laughed and said: "Go for a drink Steve, this was a great day." And he started walking away.

"But," I said, "I need to find my pack."

He laughed. "You're joking, right? It's still on your back, man, go for a drink at the bar."

It had been an afternoon shift, and all the patrollers usually went for drinks afterward. When I came in that night, after finishing paperwork, they all gave me a big cheer and even had my favourite beer waiting for me. That felt good.

In January of that year, Surrey Fire Department contacted me to come in and complete the physical. The physical was on a Saturday and the city of Surrey was about a forty-five-minute drive into the valley from my home. Apart from it being renowned as a really rough city, I didn't know much about Surrey. When I went into Hall One the morning of the test, there were already twenty other big guys there, and it was intimidating. They took my name and info, then gave me a number.

I started at the pull-up station, then went on to the sit-ups, the push-ups, and finally the stress test: riding a bike at whatever speed you could manage for twelve minutes straight, then sprint-bike for as long as you could, as hard as you could. I thought I did well, but I rode so fast I almost fell off the bike! One guy actually did fly over and they had to call an ambulance and take him to the hospital. It was intense, and I was spent.

I thought I was done when a firefighter came in and yelled my name. I walked over and he told me to follow him. We walked outside to a fully extended ladder truck — we had to climb up a hundred feet of ladder, ring the bell, and come back down. Then there was an obstacle course, a hose evaluation, and even a 150 lb dummy to carry. That last part of the testing was a complete blur. I barely remember anything aside from them saying I was done, and then vomiting several times on the way to my car.

That was my first real introduction to fire department physical testing.

Over the next three months, I got called in by Burnaby Fire, North Vancouver Fire, Delta Fire and Vancouver Fire. It seemed like every other week I was either writing an exam or doing physical testing. I had the most amazing girlfriend, and it looked like I was in enough competitions that someone would inevitably give me a chance. My life, again, had a purpose.

And then — I got the call.

It came from Surrey Fire asking me to come down to the fire hall for a meeting.

They called all fifteen candidates in and gave each of us a letter of hiring. I remember the first thing I did was call Helen and tell her. She was truly excited for me. After all those years, that skinny kid's dreams at the bus stop actually came true. This was it! Finally it was happening. I was going to be a Surrey Firefighter.

Turning twelve

The Rookie

Dating and falling in love

Too much drinking for Steve

Marrying Helen was one of the best days of my life

Our first home and my old Ford F100 pickup truck

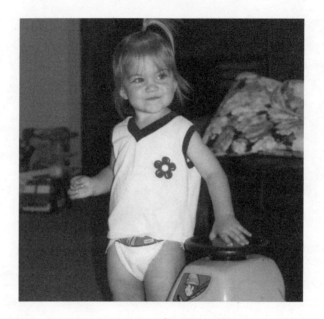

Danika was the happiest little girl on the planet

Nikolas and Woody, that doll never left his side

Bringing the kids to the firehall was always fun

The Serbic family on summer holidays at Shuswap lake

You can dress it up, but it doesn't always hide your depression

Friends again, we all got together for Mom's sixty-eighth birthday

My Dad (Deda) holding baby Nikolas

My Mom (Gramms) holding baby Nikolas.
This was the last day I spent with my mom before she passed away

CHAPTER TWELVE

Into Dark Times

As a new firefighter, I could not get enough of it! I was living my amazing dream job and the drama of my teenage years seemed safely stowed away in the past. I boxed it up and never wanted to think about it again. Living with Dad was awesome, and now my mother was back in my life. Many times she would call me slurring and saying those toxic words from the past, but I became an expert at saying, "Got to go, Mom," and quickly hanging up. My brain had become completely rewired to block the trauma from my past. My technique was a way of protecting myself against the hurtful things Mom would say when she was drinking. I was allowing only my sober mom into my life.

In my first week, we had a massive fire at the Surrey Fraser docks. It burned for five straight days and required us to work tons of overtime. The job was fascinating — much more than I ever imagined. I loved firefighting and the challenge when attending car crashes and overdoses. Sadly though, I was witnessing every possible way a person could die. The first few years in the job flew by.

I had promised myself that when I landed my dream job, I would ask Helen to marry me, and that is exactly what I did. After passing probation with Surrey Fire, and Helen landing a well-paying union job with one of the major grocery chains, we were able to finance a small home. Helen suggested that my dad move into the basement. To be honest, I would not have made that suggestion in our young marriage, even though I felt I owed it to my father. I am eternally grateful for Helen making that sacrifice.

The first few years of my career were at Fire Hall One and after applying to be an airtech, I would be there another five years. Airtech training allowed me to be called to all the large structure fires and I grew into the fire department culture quickly. Keeping my head at the beginning of my career, playing the odd practical joke, and stepping up for every volunteer opportunity gave me a sense of belonging I never felt before. Looking back, the fire service and its structure was a perfect fit for someone who carried regrets and scars from childhood. I had found my calling. I was loving life with my wife, taking care of my father, and playing hockey in the fire department two or three times a week.

I was very fortunate to have a supportive and understanding partner in Helen. When calls came at four o'clock from firefighters asking me to cover in the next hour because of some emergency, Helen never gave me a hard time. When I started out, marriages in my department had less than a fifty percent chance of survival. Early on, I became aware of the sacrifices a spouse makes to keep a marriage intact. As I had done with my childhood trauma, I became very good at boxing up dark and sad calls so as not to add stress to our relationship.

I did have one call early on that had a very strange effect on me and it took me a year before I told anyone about it. It was lunchtime and we had just sat down to eat our mexi-spuds (mashed baked potatoes, hamburger, salsa and sour cream), when a woman came into our fire hall shaking and screeching. We could not get this woman to settle down. She would not stop screaming, so the captain opened her purse and looking at her ID said, "Let's go and check out her home." I was driving and pulled the engine up to house. The front door was wide open and the captain and two guys on the back casually walked into the home. They were only in there a few minutes when Geoff came out and said, "You have to see this."

I said, "What is it?

"You have to go in and see for yourself."

So I hopped out of the driver's seat and as I stepped into the front entry, I thought I stepped on a rock, but when I lifted my foot and examined closer,

I saw it was a tooth. As I turned the corner into the kitchen the captain said, "Hey Serbic, I bet you this guy's parents always said he had no brains!"

I was looking at a body sitting in a kitchen chair holding a .30-06 rifle. There was no head on the body, just a stump of a spinal column and flaps on the shoulders that were the sides of the neck. I looked at my buddy and we were all laughing in the most bizarre way, almost like we were being forced. Police arrived and said the incident was just another argument that had ended with a suicide. We gathered our stuff and walked back to the engine, drove to the hall and everyone sat down at the fire hall galley table and stared at our mexi-spuds. The captain jumped right in and started chowing down and said, "Come on boys, eat before we get another call."

I pushed my plate away and couldn't eat anything for the rest of that day and I certainly didn't eat mexi-spuds again until years later.

My favourite fast food hamburger was usually a Wendy's Jr burger, but for some reason whenever I smelled Wendy's hamburgers, I thought of that call. A year later, I ran into one of the guys who was on the back of truck when we went to that call.

I said, "Hey Geoff, that shooting we had last year, does it bother you in any way?"

"No, not at all. Why?"

I felt weak telling him but said, "Well, whenever I smell a Wendy's burger I think about that call instantly."

He laughed and said, "There was a half-eaten hamburger and fries on the side table, didn't you see it?"

"No, I never saw it ... huh," I said.

That was the end of that conversation. Knowing that it was because I had smelled Wendy's at that call and my unconscious mind was giving me flashbacks, I started eating Wendy's burgers again. In fact, I did so the next day. I thought it was amazing that smell could trigger a flashback, but I rarely thought about that call again.

Of course, we responded to other tragic events and our department had a Critical Incident Stress Program that many firefighters used if they were having trouble processing the stuff they were seeing. After every traumatic call there was a Critical Incident Debrief session by one of the department's trained members.

I didn't like those debriefings and could never see myself needing a counsellor. I simply assumed that my childhood had given me some sort of mental tools that helped me deal with trauma better than others. All I needed was a few stiff drinks and I was always able to move on, or so I thought.

Helen was pregnant and over the next several months, the energy in our house was amazing. I was excited to become a father and when baby Nikolas arrived, it seemed life could not be going any better.

However, things started to unravel when Mom had a massive aortic aneurism and passed away. It was a very sad time. She and I had really started to become friends. A son wants to love his mother, and though it didn't happen until I was in my twenties, that love mattered very much to me.

When we went to clean out her basement suite, there were hundreds of vodka bottles everywhere. I knew she was drinking — as we became closer, she frequently called when she was drunk and I had to keep hanging up but decided that was okay as long as I kept her in my life. Face to face, she never drank in front of me when I was an adult and married. She always adamantly denied that she drank at all. The very last time I saw her, I said, "Mom can I ask you something? Are you drinking again?"

"Oh Steven, that is the medication I am on. I promise you I am not drinking." This was her usual line so I gave her a hug and those were the last words we ever spoke.

We were having Nikolas's baby shower the weekend Mom suddenly died. She had earlier declined our invitation to come and promised to send a card to our son. Four days after her death, a card arrived in the mail addressed to my son. It was written as if she knew she would never see Nikolas again:

Dear Baby Nikolas,

Here is fifty dollars. It's not enough to buy a car but hopefully when you old enough you can buy something you really want. I hope you have a wonderful life,

– Gramms

Then work got dark. Attending to a child death and two fatal car crashes really got inside my head and seemed to add to my grieving. Helen noticed I was quiet as of late and talked to me about going to see someone for some help. I really did not want to go but was having some sleepless nights and drinking wasn't as effective as usual, so I made an appointment to see a counsellor.

I told Helen I had gone and it wasn't that helpful. She asked me to go back, and I told her that counselling stuff didn't work for me, so she reluctantly let it go. I just wasn't ready.

I suppressed those feelings and didn't open up to anyone. The only thing working was four to five rum and Cokes that kept dark thoughts in their place. I didn't suffer hangovers and functioned quite normally. Over the first eight years of my career, that was my drinking pattern: two to three drinks, five times a week. It became normal — keeping me feeling okay.

We had been trying for another baby and before we knew it Helen was pregnant again Work was wearing me down a bit now and then, but with another baby on the way, I had new energy and felt very positive about our future as a family. Nikolas was now a year-and-a-half and Helen was happy.

Helen went in for her routine ultrasound at ten weeks and without any signs or warning, we were told she had miscarried. Helen went into a deep depression. Those were tough days. We didn't socialize for months but Helen slowly came around and started to get back to normal.

Then another ugly situation reared its head.

One day the phone rang. It was friend of my brother, telling me that Greg was in a bad way and we needed to get over to Vancouver Island right away. He didn't give us any details, but said it was a matter of life or death. My sister Sonya and I tried over the years to keep Greg included in our lives but he was always aloof and very hard to read. I made several phone calls and found out he had been let go from his position as a scientist in the department of fisheries. Before he left however, he threatened to come back and kill his supervisor. This was totally out of character. My brother was actually a nice guy, for the most part kind, and loved to laugh. But our family life had scarred him, and he was seriously manic at times.

We realized something was very wrong. Threatening a manager with the federal government was a serious offense, and apparently Greg was spending his time in the bars from opening until closing.

We called his family doctor and told him we needed to do a family intervention. He said he would help us because he liked my brother and knew it was a serious turn of events. We prepared what we could in advance. We called the local emergency ward, after his doctor agreed to make an assessment, so that we could then formulate a plan.

When we arrived at my brother's house in Nanaimo, he was in dire straits. He had not showered or let his dog outside for a month. There was piss and shit everywhere and Greg was covered from head-to-toe in a raw red rash. He smelled horribly, as if he was rotting from the inside out. He seemed relieved to see us, but his eyes were glazed over. He looked dead inside. My sister started crying and gave him a big hug. I started to ask how he was doing, and he just said, "Not good." He told us he was broke and his only hope was to win the 5-million-dollar jackpot on the 649 lottery. I said we were there to help him. He was silent. I asked if we could take him to the doctor, and he stayed silent. I asked several more questions without getting a response. Frustrated, I raised my voice and said, "Greg, what is the plan? What are you doing"? He responded very matter-of-factly, "Have you ever seen that movie *Leaving Las Vegas?*"

"You mean where the guy drinks himself to death?"

He answered, "Yes, I am going to drink myself to death."

We threw all his clothes into garbage bags and told him to get his shoes on. We were taking him to the doctor. After an examination, Greg confessed going to the bar at noon and drinking until it closed. Then he would go home, order a pizza, eat and throw up, go to bed and do it all over again the next day. Apparently, he had been doing this for months. He was so desperate that he kept repeating that winning the lottery was the only way out of this mess.

I made a few phone calls to people in my fire department that connected me to rehab places. We were told he had to dry out before they would take him — he was already having the DTs and shakes — we needed to get Greg into a place immediately. Finally, we found a place not far from his home that agreed to take him. We took all his clothes, got them started in the laundromat, and took him to a drug store to buy whatever he needed. Greg grabbed shaving gear, deodorant, a toothbrush and toothpaste, and four large bottles of mouthwash.

I didn't notice exactly what he had until we were at the checkout so I said, "Hey, what's with all the mouthwash, are you going to bath in the stuff?" *Whatever… he is cooperating, what do I care what he wanted to take to rehab?*

In the hours we were with him, washing his clothes and going to the drug store, Greg told us he had bought out his pension and was buying hundreds of dollars of lottery tickets every day. He said it was only a matter of time before he won the 5-million-dollar jackpot. If I heard that story one more time, I was going to lose it, but I didn't want to upset him. So I calmly said,

"Greg the odds of winning the jackpot are 1 in 14 million. It's next to impossible to win." He looked me right in the eye and said with absolute resolve,

"I will win the jackpot. You will see." I let it go. We were pulling into the parking lot of the undercover home in a very secluded area. People were waiting in the driveway for us. It was intimidating. They walked us into the home and as one guy started searching through the bags. A big burly guy told us we needed to leave now. Just as he said that, the other guy pulled out the bottles of mouthwash and looked at my brother and said, "You're fucking joking, right?" and laughed.

"What is going on?" I asked.

"Did you know he had the mouthwash?"

"Yes, I bought all that stuff."

He laughed and said, "You have never been to detox obviously. Your brother is going to drink this shit mouthwash that is 65% alcohol." Greg looked at the ground in shame while the big burly guy said in a firm voice, "Time to leave folks." My sister was crying. We turned and walked out.

That was the beginning of two years of hell, with Greg in and out of rehab and recovery, calling me frequently in a manic state, threating to kill himself. He even explained to me exactly how he was going to do it with a drink he could make in seconds that would kill him in minutes.

It was an exhausting phase and certain calls at work started to affect me. I was tired and drinking more. I felt like the world was spinning too fast with one day evaporating into the next.

During one of the darkest times dealing with my brother, Helen told me she was pregnant again. We talked about our future as a family and Helen said she was worried because my brother was consuming me with his negativity and threats. She wanted me to help him but thought I was getting pushed and pulled.

One day my brother called me, and he was not in a good mood. He told me I had the perfect life and that I didn't understand how much pain he was in.

As always, I said, "I am trying to understand, and I want to help you." The more I said, the angrier he became, yelling that no one understands him. Then he said, "If you come home from work and find Helen and your son Nikolas stabbed multiple times in a blood-spattered room, then you will understand how I feel."

I paused. I took a deep breath, thought about my wife and family, the upcoming birth of a new baby, and said, "Greg, I love you, but I can't do this anymore." I hung up the phone.

The next day Greg's friend called and said something had happened and Greg was in the ICU at Nanaimo General Hospital. Sonya and I drove to the ferry and raced to the hospital where Greg was intubated and in a coma. I asked the emergency doctor if he thought it was a failed suicide attempt, and he asked me why. I told him, in a confrontation over the phone, that my brother had threatened to take his own life by drinking toilet bowl cleaner mixed with another household product. The emergency doctor said that made sense because my brother was unconscious when the ambulance brought him in, and his blood acid level was off the charts.

After thirty-eight days on a respirator, the doctor said that Greg's condition was terminal. His organs were shutting down. We needed to make the decision to disconnect him from life support. It was difficult, but we agreed it was best to take him off life support. I held his hand. I apologized for what I said on the phone. His breathing shallowed. Within the hour, he passed away. Greg was forty-six years old.

On the trip home from the hospital, I reflected on our childhood, feeling grateful for the laughter and fun times Greg and I had shared. I thought about the few years right up until our last words spoken and of the moment he took his final breath. I felt hollowed out inside, empty. The trip back to the mainland was eternal.

One of my fears about my brother's funeral was that no one would show up. Like so many families, we did not want to tell anyone or even admit to ourselves the challenges Greg went through, or that he took his own life.

About fifty people showed including friends from school and old neighbours. The day gave us closure. One neighbour I wasn't expecting showed up. She had really disliked me as a kid because I tormented them, stealing all their Christmas lights, tying fishing line from their car to their garbage cans so when they drove off to work in the morning they would be followed down the road by their two garbage cans — stupid stuff I did just to piss them off. I was surprised and relieved when this same neighbour came up and gave me a massive hug and told me how proud she was of what I had become. She said all the neighbours figured I would end up getting involved in crime and drugs and were so happy I had turned out well. I was relieved.

As the next few months went by, I felt so positive about our future as a family. Helen's pregnancy was going well and we were full of happiness and excitement.

While we were both hoping for a girl, Helen and I just prayed for a safe delivery. Thankfully, that is exactly what happened, and our beautiful baby girl Danika Marie (my mom's middle name was Marie) was born.

Then after a decade on the job, the shit really hit the fan when I had a series of bad calls and baby Danika became deathly ill. After a complete meltdown, I finally sought counselling.

CHAPTER THIRTEEN

Clinical Counselling and Changing my Perspective

Getting my childhood dream job as a firefighter was life changing and an amazing fit for me. I loved being a firefighter! It was everything I imagined it to be. I won the lottery with that job. Upon reflection, perhaps the only thing lacking was training and education about the effects of seeing trauma on a regular basis. It might have been one of the most important things to learn before beginning my career; though without any on-the-job experience, would I have understood it in advance? I realize now how I mismanaged my mental health and am grateful for the help of some amazing professionals who gave me the tools to process healing.

Opening up to clinical counselling was a new way of understanding why I react and respond to trauma the way I do. Learning self-care with Teresa, one of the best clinical counsellors I had during my career, was truly beneficial. She really knew how to handle first responders. When I told her I did not want to go back and revisit my childhood, she just said, *Okay*. I told her I wanted to deal with the trauma I had just seen and wanted help getting through the immediate issues I was struggling with — the anxiety, insomnia, and self-medicating with alcohol. Teresa agreed, and introduced me to the 'Stop Sign' technique, designed to help the flashbacks and nightmares subside. She asked me to close my eyes and describe in detail what a stop sign looks like, and then open my eyes and draw it on her flip chart. Every time

I had a flashback, she said, "Close your eyes and think about every detail of that stop sign; and if you can draw it, that's even better."

When a first responder, like myself, connects with a clinical counsellor and finds the ability to trust enough to open up to talk therapy, we all do the same thing. We unload twenty years of built-up baggage and expect instant results. Once we connect with a counsellor and start to see progress, we open up completely. That's what I did. Teresa asked me to look back in time, something I never wanted to do. I blocked the past from my memory because I had a great wife, great kids — I was worried that reflecting on the earlier troubles of my life could affect my *current* fantastic life, as if dwelling on my dysfunctional childhood could somehow sabotage that. Frankly, I was terrified and embarrassed to go there but Teresa was different than any counsellor I had met. I could trust her. Internalizing the shame of my childhood for so long had suffocated my adult life. But Teresa was one of the few people that intuitively knew how to reach me.

After our initial sessions, I began to talk about my childhood unsolicited. Haunted by regret and shame, I believed it played a part in my inability to sleep. Teresa said that my past had nothing to do with the trauma witnessed in my career — those were two very different challenges. My childhood was in the past, she said. It was my perception of the past that needed tackling. She explained that my childhood was not the reason for sleeping poorly or pounding back the booze — it was hanging onto my *beliefs* about the past that was the problem. Teresa gave me some homework to write down all the things I felt shameful and regretful about. I needed to learn to control my thoughts to manage my feelings. She reminded me that like everyone else, it was natural to fixate on negative thoughts, especially those we can't rationalize. For me, she said, the events I didn't understand just went round-and-round in my head. To gain control, I had to fight hard to stop thinking about them. It's important to understand that traumatic events are still there, even if you think you have them successfully blocked from your memory. They can come crashing back into one's life at any time, and probably when it is least convenient.

Teresa was insistent that I write down only the issues bothering me, and at the same time, start remembering the things in childhood that brought me joy. She wanted me to relish the fun times and positives, not so much to record them on paper, but to keep them in mind. As human beings, we have to train ourselves to accept the negative experiences and promote the positive ones in our lives. Before we can do that, she said, we have to bring the positives to the surface, as we tend to forget them. Most people only remember the terrible, negative stuff from their past and it accumulates over time. In her opinion, the negative experiences from my childhood had built up and my arduous career choice had compounded them in the core of my being.

In another session, Teresa asked me about my family relationships. I explained that of all the tensions growing up in my house, the most stressful thing, aside from my mother's drinking problem, was that my brother *despised* my father. He blamed my father for every single problem, every downfall in his life. He absolutely hated my dad, and they never spoke. To have two people living in the same house who never spoke to each other made day-to-day life very tense.

Teresa asked if I thought my mother loved my father. I said she always made him feel like shit whenever she had the opportunity. So no, I didn't think she loved him. My father, on the other hand, still loved my mom. It destroyed him that she was a drunk. I'm certain it was part of his own reason for drinking. He may have been difficult to be married to for one reason or another, but I never saw it. Maybe it was because I didn't want to, but he seemed to be a good man. I could tell when he looked at her, and talked about the good old days, she was special to him and he still loved her.

My family had so much potential, but ended up such a disaster and embarrassment, and I played a huge part in that, being such a troublemaker. By the time I was about ten years old, I used to pray that I could go live with another family, even dreaming about it when I went to bed.

Then Teresa asked, "What do you think might have changed your family and helped you to all become closer?"

"If we could have changed where we lived, for one thing," I said. "We lived in a very low-income area filled with crime. I don't know what happened to my mother and father before I was born for them to get to where they were — but they were such nice, caring people when they weren't drinking."

"If your family was closer and happier do you think you would have gotten into trouble like you did?

"No way, I would have been a much better kid for sure."

"Would you feel the same, if your family lived in the low-income neighbourhood, but were much closer?"

I could see where she was going, and I bit.

I said, "I felt we would have been an amazing, far closer family without the drinking — one hundred percent."

"Do you think you could have controlled or changed that?" Teresa asked.

"I don't think so … it was happening as far back as I can remember. I was just a little kid that no one listened to … so, no."

Teresa let me answer in a specific way, showing me that it wasn't my fault. I had no control over my family, so I needed to get over it. This woman had me dialed in and pushed my buttons perfectly, so that I walked right into her questions already armed with the answers I needed to tell myself.

It's funny how simply talking, simply opening up to someone, can change your mental state. I was also relieved that I wasn't going crazy, that there was hope. Although my wife and I can talk about anything after years of unloading my negativity on her, I eventually felt like too much of a 'pity party.' She was always supportive — don't get me wrong — but I felt like I was actually losing my mind and didn't want her to see that. When you fall into that kind of depression, you feel infectiously weak and, to be honest, like a total loser.

With Teresa's guidance, I learned the importance of forgiveness. I am the one who kept the memories of my dysfunctional family alive and well. I blamed Mom and Dad for everything, when in many ways, they were struggling — it wasn't their fault. Teresa showed me how my parents were good people by focusing on the positive things that happened in my life. She taught me how to let go of all the stuff I felt was so bad. I changed my perception of childhood, taking what I had envisioned as toxic and dark as not so bad after all—in fact pretty darn good in a lot of ways. Learning how to forgive was massive for me to grow into a new positive lifestyle. Yes, I needed to forgive my parents, but I also had to forgive myself. I hurt people, stole, and broke into places at such a young age and was ashamed, but again that was my perception of the past. I just needed to change my thinking around to rid myself of the guilt and shame.

With the tools I had now acquired, including writing down the story of my life, Teresa believed I could control my thoughts. By controlling my thoughts, I could control the direction of my life while improving my mental health and resiliency.

I went back to work, feeling like a dump truck had been lifted off my shoulders. For the first time since my mental meltdown, I felt normal. We were super busy, but nothing came up that was too spectacular or horrifying. I continued to do what Teresa suggested, writing those issues I did not want to think about down on paper — really having no idea why. The only thing she had left me with was, "You will see." Indeed, *I did see* when I attended a post-traumatic stress retreat many years later.

The next several years of my career were solid. I had the tools and was able to process trauma, thanks to Teresa. Taking that journey, the most important thing I learned is *its okay to not be okay* after seeing an event you can't make any sense of; and that self-medicating only makes things worse.

The shock of 9/11

I am getting Nikolas ready for kindergarten and Danika set to drop off at daycare when my phone rings. It's Helen on my display. She is crying and tells me to turn on the TV. I ask what's wrong and she shouts at me to turn on the news. I am terrified because she is so upset.

I am shocked by what I see. Filling the screen is live footage of a passenger plane crashing into the north tower of the World Trade Centre at 8:46 am, leaving a huge hole with heavy smoke and fire pouring from the building. I feel sick to my stomach.

My neighbour Kath called and asked why I was late. I told her what was happening and she came by and grabbed the kids. Then I watched as the second plane hit the south tower about fifteen minutes later. I remained transfixed when another plane hit the Pentagon, and less than an hour after the initial hit, the collapse of the south tower followed by the north tower at 10:28 am.

Within a day, the call went out for assistance from firefighters across North America, and my department began sending members within the first few days. I flew from Vancouver to New York City in early October 2001 and joined another 10,000 firefighters who had come to help. I found myself walking down a dust-filled street towards what looked like a gigantic termite mound with steel building frames sticking out of the top. Incredibly bright emergency lights continuously lit the still smoldering site. A peculiar burning smell cut into my nostrils.

After walking several blocks, we arrived at Firehouse 10, and a captain from FDNY whacked me on the shoulder as he went by saying, "Thanks for coming boys. This is war!" motioning with his thumb to the collapsed north tower that was still burning. My buddies and I stood watching as FDNY members dug out their brothers on hands and knees. They carried a mummified brother right by us. We had only been on the ground a couple of hours and stood there in shock. Then one of my buddies saluted, so I brought my shaking hand up to my head and did the same. We were standing on the gigantic mound of dirt (or what I thought was dirt) just staring and a FDNY firefighter walked up and introduced himself. We exchanged pleasantries and then he asked what I was seeing in that moment. As if it was a trick question, I asked him to repeat it. I still had no idea where he was going with this. I was in total shock after watching it all on TV and now I was standing at the base of the still burning one hundred and ten story tower that was fully collapsed in front of me, looking into a smoky sky saying, "What the fuck is happening?" He snapped me out of it by saying, "Steve, there is no fucking dirt in uptown, brother. That is not dirt — the building completely pulverized," He said it so absolutely, like he was an engineer. "Look around, try and find one piece of glass or concrete — you won't brother, because it's all dust."

He was right. Every day when we entered the secured area and walked the several blocks to the pile, the dust was knee high in some places. We went to the pile and walked right by the three storefronts converted to a morgue — and every day the two piles grew higher with the flattened air packs and bottles the firefighters carried on their backs, and the turn-out gear they were wearing. Every day, FDNY brothers dug another brother from the rubble. When they got close to a buried body, they dug with their hands so as not to cause more damage.

As Canadian firefighters, we were not allowed to work at the pile although thousands of firefighters were there that week wanting to do something — anything to help. Ground zero was a crime scene controlled by the FBI. We were allowed to come every night, as if coming to a shrine to pay our respects and go into Firehouse 10 and chat with crews and other firefighters. Some of the guys rode trucks who had lost firefighters in the attacks and asked us to please attend as many of the daily funeral services as we could. The funerals were all different. The service we attended at the Far Rockaways was one among a dozen other funerals that day with only 80 people attending and half of us were from Canada. This particular firefighter had only been on the job 10 months.

The FDNY guys told us stories like dropping the new rookie off on the street on the way to the towers, so they would survive. Bodies being pulled out with social security numbers penned on their arms for identification because they knew they were going to die. One of the most amazing stories was about the crew from Ladder Co. 6 who survived the collapse due to what they believed was divine intervention. After receiving orders to do a search and rescue of the north tower, Ladder Company 6 went up on foot, making it to the 27th floor. Heading down the stairs, they found a woman named Josephine Harris on the 20th floor who could not walk on her own. They refused to leave her behind and carried her down the twenty flights of stairs, making it to the fourth floor as the north tower started collapsing. When the collapse ended, there were a dozen people in that stairwell, all completely unhurt, but trapped. Eventually, the crew made it out of the rubble and rescued the others in the stairwell.

Most evenings after attending funeral services, we ended up walking around Times Square with thousands of other firefighters from all over North America. Going into a bar was amazing. New Yorkers bought us drinks and said how grateful they were that we had come to help; though I didn't feel we were doing enough being in a bar when crews at that same moment were down at the pile digging. We all felt that way about wanting to work but the FDNY needed us for emotional support for the funerals of the many firefighters who lost their lives. A New Yorker told me she felt much safer when the city was flooded with uniformed personnel after September 11. That made me happy and I felt better about being there attending funerals for those fallen firefighters I never had the honour of meeting.

I was still uncomfortable with people buying us drinks all the time in the Times Square bars, so one night after attending that day's funerals, my buds and I went to a bar called the Slaughtered Lamb in Greenwich Village. It was about 10 pm and we quietly sat and talked as the small bar started to fill with a group of locals. By 11 pm, the place was packed, and sure enough, the wave of drinks came. I asked the bartender to point out who had sent the last round. I headed over to a couple in the corner to say thank you. I spent the whole night talking with them. That is what happened every time, because their stories were fascinating. I mentioned how guilty I felt about random people buying us drinks and one of the fellows responded by telling me what had happened to him.

He said he was on the seventieth floor of the north tower when the plane hit. He and thousands of people jammed the stairwells heading down because the elevators were unusable, filled with aviation fuel and fire. It took forever to get down the stairwell and he thought he was going to die for sure. He said he saw the faces of the amazing firefighters climbing the stairs in the other direction, heading into the fire and the chaos, all of which he believed never made it back out. When he got close to the lobby, he was panicking, just wanting to be out of the building, but the crowd heading down the stairs stopped moving. They were on a skybridge that joined the two towers, and he could see down into the ground floor courtyard between the two towers. One firefighter was standing there alone looking up. Then he heard a loud roar and a rumble, and the whole lobby area started shaking. He said the entire crowd was watching that firefighter who was now running when a massive piece of debris crashed to the ground exactly where the firefighter had stood. The entire crowd started to scream and got moving again. When he finally made it outside, there was a huge crowd standing there looking up. He remembers a woman holding a baby, just watching, and said he will never forget the number of spectators. He ran for over twenty blocks until he could not run anymore — then he turned around and just watched. Once the south tower fell, he walked home and ever since has never looked in that direction of the city. Finally, he said, "If I want to buy you a drink because it makes me feel better, you better let me." I just said okay, but before I left, I wanted to give this man something. I had my full-dress uniform on and asked him if I could give him my uniform shirt and he said no. So I ripped the flashing off my shoulder, gave it to him, and went to shake his hand but he stood up and gave me a hug. I brought six uniform shirts. After eight days I came home with none. And I gave away all my shoulder flashings.

A total of 343 firefighters lost their lives doing their job on 9/11. Even though we firefighters say we are prepared to do our job no matter what the cost, we don't ever go to work thinking it is going to be our last day on the planet. When 9/11 happened, every firefighter felt instantly humbled and most of us wanted to help in any way we could with so many people buried underground. In the end, authorities were only able to find and match DNA from 60% of the victims, leaving 1109 people unidentified. I will never forget it.

Three of my group who went to New York became sick. I had a tumour against the carotid artery in my head and had surgery to remove half of it. One is in remission for prostate cancer, and another is currently in remission for non-Hodgkin's lymphoma. I am not saying our illnesses had anything to do with being at ground zero during 9/11, or if we became sick because of our exposures doing our regular jobs as firefighters. I do know we all feel deep compassion for those FDNY members who went to that toxic pile every day and dug without ever questioning the cost to their health. I have followed all the congressional roadblocks put before first responders demanding continued health care benefits for those who fought to save so many others that fateful day in 2001. Thank you, Jon Stewart. You put those fucking politicians in their place, when they talked from behind their desks as if they were there. The firefighters around the world also thank you, Jon, and the first responders who helped get those FDNY families the support they are entitled to receive. That struggle finally ended in July 2019 when President Donald Trump was compelled to sign a bill that permanently reauthorized the September 11th Victim Compensation Fund, which pays out claims for deaths and illnesses related to the attack through to 2090.

After my mid-career meltdown, followed by 9/11, I looked at things differently. The firefighters who lost their lives on September 11th elevated the heroism of the fire culture to its highest level. Departments were signing contracts wherein danger pay was now considered, not just for dying on the job, but for job-related cancers. The sacrifice of those men and women on that tragic day helped hundreds of firefighters live healthier and safer lives.

And I was so glad to have the tools and understanding Teresa gave me to process trauma because one of the worst calls I ever responded to occurred later in 2004.

The Hanging

The crew was just completing truck checks after starting our shift when the tones went off, "Engine 12: report of a residential structure fire…" We responded quickly to find a home full of smoke and a small fire in the basement that we quickly extinguished —simple knockdown. We did a thorough check for extension and when confident the fire was completely extinguished, we returned to the fire hall. Our paid on-call firefighters stayed behind to do a two-hour fire watch.

After about a half-hour getting the trucks back in service, loading hose and cleaning up the tools we used, we all hopped back on the engine to drive to the home to do one last check and relieve the on-call firefighters.

We were about half-way to the home when Engine 13 gets a tone over the radio for "a hanging." We were only two blocks away while driving down the road that separated our two response zones. We told dispatch we'd take the call and would be there in less than a minute.

Arriving at the address, there was no one around, so we pounded on the front door and looked through the windows but could not see anyone. I walked back out to the street and saw a couple of teenagers halfway down the block, so I yelled at them to come over. They ran closer and told us to look though the little window next to the front door. It was hard to see clearly through the sheer curtain but it appeared someone was hanging right in front of the window. We booted in the door and were accosted by that smell that first responders never forget —the smell of a person who has been deceased for some time in a heated room. That odour seeps into your clothes and through to your skin and only an immediate hot shower alleviates the stench.

There was nothing we could do. We are required to leave the person in the state we find them for investigation purposes. I told the rookie that was with us to go back to the truck with the driver and I would go in and check the rest of the house. In the old days, I always kept a container of Vicks VapoRub in my jacket. I wipe some under my nose to cover the foul smell of the deceased so my gag reflex would not trigger. This time, I didn't have it on me, so I took a huge deep breath and quickly walked into the house, through the kitchen and living room and exhaled as I ran up the stairs to the bedrooms. The first door I opened was a kid's room, a teenage girl, I guessed, as pop posters on the walls and the clothes in the closet confirmed it. The bed was messy, and someone had clearly slept there. As I walked down the hall, I could see a set of double doors and assumed it was the master bedroom. When I opened that door, what I saw will stay with me forever.

Placed in the bed was the wife and daughter. They had clearly been murdered, and then dressed. They had the same thick make-up on each of their faces. Their eyes were open and looking straight at me. I froze, standing there and staring back into their eyes as my mind calculated what to do. It was like there were spirits in the room with me. The hair on my neck stood on end, it was the weirdest feeling I have ever encountered at a call. I snapped out of the eye lock from the mom and daughter in bed and grabbed my radio mic asking for dispatch to update police that multiple bodies were in the home. Dispatch came back with, "Say again Engine 12 …"

I repeated, "There are multiple bodies in this home."

As soon as they heard that over the radio, the crew came running into the crime scene. I yelled to them to get out of the house. I walked out of the room towards them and down the stairs, pushing them in front of me, and exited the home as fast as we could. Outside, there was a neighbour demanding to know what was going on. I could barely understand what he was saying, as if I was under water and struggling to catch my breath. Then a female police officer arrived and asked me to show her the scene. I suggested that she wait for another member to arrive but she didn't seem bothered and said no one else was coming — all the units were busy. We walked up the stairs and through the double doors and I didn't look at the deceased again. I just focused on the police officer's face and though I had warned her of what we had, she was clearly unprepared for what she saw.

I had nightmares about that call. But I acted on Teresa's advice to go and see someone as soon as possible when having trouble processing a bad call. I quickly got in to see a psychologist. He was a former police officer, and was not Teresa, but we connected well. He worked with me to understand all the aspects of the call; then the nightmares stopped, and I was okay.

He diagnosed me with PTSD and put it in my medical file. I knew this event was hard to process, not because I had PTSD, but because I mismanaged my trauma by over-medicating with alcohol, which was affecting my ability to sleep. As much as I liked that psychologist, I did not want that PTSD diagnosis in my medical file, and he would not budge on that request. I felt we were no longer connecting, and I moved on.

It's not that I didn't appreciate this new psychologist experience, but since working with Teresa I felt differently about dealing with trauma, and I wanted to fight against accepting that I had a mental disorder.

I wasn't disordered, I was injured from witnessing horrific events.

Teresa had taught me to get my head around the trauma to be able to recover. Going to clinical counselling is more about understanding yourself, and your triggers. Just as physiotherapy helps heal a pulled muscled, clinical counselling helps an injured mind so you can wrap your head around what you saw. The aftermath of a murder is extremely difficult to process. But if you park it or block it, your duffle bag will eventually fill up and spill out like it did for me.

It wasn't my childhood memories or the bad calls, it was the fact that I blocked them. And whenever something came out, I drank it away until the day the flood gates opened.

I ended up leaving Surrey Fire as a firefighter, only to come back full circle many years later as a chief officer.

In the midst of that challenge, I met Ken.

CHAPTER FOURTEEN

Embrace the Change

As Assistant Chief at Esquimalt Fire, I was so fortunate to meet Ken Gill and get to know and work with him for three years. When Ken took his own life in 2018, it hit me hard. I grieved intensely for him and his family. And then I grew angry for a long time, upset by the fact that I had missed the signs. We had spoken about suicidal thoughts when we first met and continued to build our relationship around the topic of mental health and depression, but I was unaware that he was struggling towards the end. Ken was a man who wanted to help people, a man of strong faith who, despite his own depression and suicidal thoughts, was able to provide support and assistance to hundreds of firefighters. Ken was always so "on" and kept any sign of depression well hidden. It is very hard to read the signs, and I and no other firefighter saw them in Ken.

Ken really battled hard. Then when he was finally in care at the hospital in Victoria, the psychiatrists on duty kept changing his drug protocol, and the change in doctors and drugs prevented Ken from coming out of that dark depression which ultimately cost him his life.

After a few months, my anger lessened, and I was able to realize how Ken's death helped me discover a gift from trauma — the courage to be vulnerable. He guided me to a place in my life where I can help others and take care of myself at the same time. I will never forget him. I will carry on what he inspired in me — the courage to step up and tell my whole story.

Six months after Ken's death, I was fortunate to attend the BC First Responders Resiliency Program. It is a unique program initiated in 2017 after several Surrey firefighters died by suicide in 2015. Along with eight other fire chiefs, I participated in the four-day program at Loon Lake in Maple Ridge, BC, conducted by doctors and peer support counsellors specializing in post-traumatic stress and job-related mental health issues. More than one-hundred firefighters have been through this program and it has received rave reviews.

One of our initial tasks was to write down our childhood experiences up until the time we became firefighters. The doctor said we were not expected to speak about these experiences, but just to write them down. I did not let them know I had done this before in my counselling sessions with Teresa and was not interested in telling my story to this group, but I went ahead and wrote it down. Then they did something that gave my former counselling experience complete clarity. It was like a lightning bolt when they took our stories and had us literally rip out the negative parts and throw them away. For the exceptionally bad childhood experiences, we were encouraged to burn them. Teresa told me I needed to let the negatives from my past go, and this was exactly what she meant. It was as if I could hear her voice as I sat with that group of fire chiefs: "You now have your negative childhood experiences on paper, it is only your perception that is bad, but it does not own you. So, let it go. You have been dragging an anchor around your whole life because you are choosing to. It is in the past, not in the now, so you need to make a choice. You can put it on a shelf where it will keep haunting you, or you can mentally rid yourself of the negative childhood memories. You are the only one who can let them go. Let them go, Steve."

I held onto my past because it justified so many things — sadness, anger, drinking —which ultimately prevented me from living unattached happiness. What I have learned through my journey is how important it is to deal with your past mentally, not by reliving it, but changing your perception of it.

Your childhood, relationships, and any trauma you have struggled with, no matter how insignificant they may seem, are incredibly important to examine with the guidance of a health professional you can trust. A skilled therapist can get into your head and help to change your perspective on how you see things. You will learn to look at them positively as opportunities for growth and healing. When you understand how depression, ADHD, PTSI, concussions or other physical injuries may also affect your ability to process trauma, you will learn coping mechanisms to live in the now — the past does not have to drive the future.

The past is the past.

As an Assistant Chief when I participated in the Resiliency Program, one of the things that I always struggled with was calming down when arriving at a stressful event like a car crash with fatalities or fires with people trapped. One of the doctors at this retreat showed us some tactical breathing techniques, one being box breathing, as a way to control heart rhythm. I asked one of the clinical counsellors if he could recommend a doctor that could teach me more about this breathing technique. He gave me the name of a doctor who lived not far from my home. We did about ten sessions and before I knew it, I could control my anxiety and my fight-or-flight impulse quickly with a simple breathing technique that combined breathing with visualizations. Here is the crazy thing — this technique has been around for thousands of years and is the basis of yoga and meditation, but the fire service had never employed it for incident commanders. I began to spread the word, and it is now a big part of my ESM (Emergency Scene Management) Protocols as one of the most powerful and effective tools out there to manage stress.

It is unrealistic to think that every day of your life is going to be amazing, but what I learned at that retreat is that you can point yourself in the right direction. Each person has their own factory setting — understanding what that is will help you start your day on a positive note. I have implemented several techniques that enable me to face each day. A good night's sleep and a healthy diet goes a long way, as well as finding something to motivate you in the morning — for me it is gratitude. Adding controlled breathing in advance of a perceived stressful event assists in preparation for dealing with any anticipated challenge a firefighter may face. The combination of understanding the need for REM sleep, controlled breathing, and gratitude are the critical components in my daily routine that have made a significant impact in my life.

Changing the culture

Firefighters are the toughest occupational athletes on the planet. Until they are not. Changing the fire service culture is to realize that no one is immune to the emotional and mental health issues that develop from regularly dealing with emergencies. It is not an easy task to make change but it is important to establish an environment wherein everyone—from the top down to new recruits—is trained to understand the signs of mental health issues firefighters struggle with for fear of being stigmatized as weak and unfit to do their jobs. An environment where members feel understood and supported and unafraid to admit they may be troubled and wish to seek counselling will go a long way in reducing substance abuse, depression, and potential suicide. Support and educational services should be extended to a member's spouse and children. Families are often kept in the dark, with no idea of what post-traumatic stress injuries look like and why a firefighter may be engaging in self-destructive behavior.

The fire department has always been a culture with very little room for mistakes without getting ripped and embarrassed by your peers, and that component still exists today. It needs to change! Some suicides in the fire service have been linked to intimidation, and a lack of acceptance for failures, common in the culture, but not easy to identify and tackle by any organization. An IAFF survey of 7000 firefighters indicated that 81% said if they reached out for help, they would be thought of as weak or unfit for duty. That stigma needs to be addressed immediately. It is costing us lives.

I have given talks about mental health awareness to thousands of firefighters and the feedback received is commonly a comment such as, "the department doesn't understand." In my role as a chief officer having many discussions with members, I do not feel the messages are making their way up the chain. Their complaints are commonly made at firehouse floor level but not reaching the people who need to hear them. A better forum is required where every firefighter who needs support or just wants to be heard can find a way to speak, no matter what their rank. I have learned a lot over the last few years and have grown immensely. I am a different person now and look forward to making a difference when it comes to mental health in the fire service.

Fire departments from the 1970s to 90s used to promote socializing after firefighter shifts. Why were PTSI claims so much lower in those days? Was it because there was less trauma and fires? No, there were ten times more fires in most cities, but having a get-together after work gave you the opportunity to speak up about something you may not have mentioned in the fire hall. In those days, alcohol was a large part of that social bonding and having a few drinks can be helpful to give some of us the courage to speak up. Once you started talking, it got even easier. Getting together for a few beers and bonding as a crew through talk and laughter was cathartic. It was a kind of "organizational clinical counselling" of itself before fire departments had other resources and it was effective in its own way.

It's hard to pinpoint exactly what has changed. I honestly believe that the loss of camaraderie and the opportunities to bond as we used to are missing today. The first step to breaking down the stigma is to have unpressured, easy, open conversation with the entire crew at that galley table during lunch, dinner or some other venue after work. Seeing one of your peers get emotional is extremely powerful in building up crew support, resiliency, and morale. Seeing someone with the same struggles you may be having is reassuring that you are not alone. An open-door policy is also a must when it comes to supporting crews with mental health issues and helping fellow members process traumatic calls when they want privacy from their peers. Being able to stay on shift while receiving clinical counselling is proven to benefit firefighters recovering from PTSI. Special dinners at the hall, meeting for dinner or drinks a couple of times a month, weekly sports, hunting or biking trips can be huge in building crew camaraderie and morale.

Fire culture has been evolving over the last decade, eroding pillars in some areas and making strides in others. Positive changes are shaping up across North America with fitness and mental health arising as priority initiatives to building better working environments. Programs are underway to better prevent workplace injury, cardiovascular disease risk, and deterioration of mental health. Government presumptive legislation has been amended to cover more presumptive diseases like cancer under the Workers Compensation Act for firefighters.

Like many firefighters (aware of the dangers), being hired for the job was the best thing that happened to me. So what transpired over the last decade? Did we forget why we took an oath and what our purpose is in our cities and communities? Has the loss of our brothers and sisters to suicide contributed to the increased numbers of mental health claims?

Fifty years ago, half of a fire department's calls were structure fire calls but today those types of calls are below 3% of the call volume. Now calls are mostly medical, false alarms, vehicle incidents, and rescues. In big cities, up to 75% of the calls relate to mental health or overdose situations. We have very little training when it comes to dealing with patients with mental illness; so while we may not be at risk for building collapse when we go to a call, we are at risk for a mental health injury.

Looking back, with the help of a clinical counsellor and talk therapy, I realized that I suffered from several post-traumatic stress injuries as a child and as a firefighter. I did not have a mental disorder. Through that clinical counselling, I was able to release my past and find the power of self-acceptance and vulnerability. It was the game changer for me — simple and powerful. If you are willing to be open and vulnerable, you can benefit from all that talk therapy has to offer. It is there for you. You just need to be courageous enough to do some self-examination. It is school, and the subject is yourself, your life habits, thoughts, and your reactions to them. All current research clearly demonstrates that cognitive behavioral therapy is the most efficacious. In basic terms, providing the client with training on how to "think" differently about trauma will reduce the symptoms of PTSI.

My experience and what I went through is not limited to first responders. Depression and alcohol abuse almost cost me everything, including my life. Looking back, I know it was because I was not trained nor equipped to handle that downward spiral. I know that now and wish I had learned this earlier in my career.

I have lost people I care about to suicide and there is an epidemic happening right now. More firefighters take their own lives than die in the line of duty; more than ten times the suicide rate of the general public. What got me through my mental health crash was a supportive family, friends, and an amazing clinical therapist. It is unfortunate that many people do not know how to access critical resources and subsequently do not make it. Combined with the common practice of GPs prescribing anti-depressants without first referring the patient to a clinical counsellor only serves to mask depression and potentially weaken mental health.

When I was struggling, sleep dysfunction, alcohol abuse, and the feelings of hopelessness as well as retracting from people who cared about me kept me in a psychosis. A number of firefighters who reached out to me for help are grappling with the same issues—sleep, drugs, and alcohol abuse, used as coping mechanisms that I too thought would get me through it. I was wrong. It didn't work for me and won't work for them either in the long run.

I feel so fortunate to have served as a professional firefighter. I started my career thinking I was bullet proof — someone who would never be affected by a post-traumatic stress injury. The loss of my brother was my first exposure to suicide and learning how to deal with and process losing someone to mental illness and recovering from my own struggles in the past, I have a better understanding of what happens to a person's mind when they get into that dark valley and all seems to be lost. We know that suicide intervention is possible if we can recognize when someone is suicidal. We must do better at finding ways to identify and support our firefighters by having resources available. The fire service culture may never completely accept a firefighter's need to talk openly about depression and having suicidal thoughts at the galley table, but we are slowly making progress.

The fire service opened many doors for me. And as I reflect back to the day I sat at that bus stop in East Vancouver so many years ago, surrounded by the bruised and broken members of a community overlooked by many, and caught the smile of the firefighter who proudly served that community, I wonder if he realized what he did for one lost youth. I feel like I have become him, that he was always within me. The journey, the ups-and-downs are what propelled me to become stronger and more resilient and without that adversity I would not be who I am today.

Today, I am proud to say I finally know who I am. I have changed the way I think and feel about life in a manner that has truly made me healthier and happier. I am able to forgive myself for the things I have done and the mistakes I have made. I am also able to forgive others. I was the one who kept the memories of having a dysfunctional family alive and well my whole life. I blamed my mom and dad for everything that happened to me — I took ownership of nothing. The toughest part of this whole process was admitting to myself that I have depression. Once I did, I could finally understand and manage my sadness allowing me to continue the rest of my journey unbroken.

Life is school, as we move through our journey of life, we learn. I thought finding the perfect person to spend the rest of my life with, my dream job, and to be given two amazing kids would have grounded me to a safe and stable life.

I could not have been more mistaken. The greatest challenge of my life was yet to come.

When this book was published, Steve Serbic was an Assistant Fire Chief of Operations with one of the busiest fire departments in the country. That skinny little boy with no self-esteem in that learning assistance class four and half decades ago would be very proud of who he became.

Watch for Steve's second book in 2022.

ACKNOWLEDGEMENTS

I began this book over a decade ago and would never have completed it without the constant support and encouragement from my wife Helen. We have been together for many years and she has helped me get up off my knees countless times. Thank you, Helen, for being in my life and accepting me for who I am. Nik and Dani, you are the greatest two kids any father could have asked for. You are my strength.

Of course, this book was also not possible without inspiration from my friend Ken Gill. I am particularly grateful to his wife Marie for sharing her thoughts about Ken's struggle with depression. And I wish to thank the input of Dr. Chuck whose expertise counselling veterans and firefighters has led me to a deeper understanding of why suicide (in some cases) is the only way to end the pain of prolonged depression.

Having a friend like Dr. Jim Keats who has helped me personally and dedicated his life to helping people who have suffered trauma, the majority of them firefighters, has been a blessing when it came to writing this book.

Thank you, Dr. Debbie, for helping me through my toughest days. You saved my life.

I am grateful for the assistance of Sonya talking about our childhood, Anita for being there when I needed help with writing, editing and feedback on parts of this book. Your time and conversation gave me much needed clarity. Colton, for helping me at the start of this project, to get organized and for convincing me to get an editor. To my editor, Eve Chapple, I am sincerely appreciative of your patience and dedication in constructing a coherent narrative. To Lori Yohannes, my final pair of eyes, I can't thank you enough for taking my manuscript from what it was to what it is. I am so excited to have you as my editor for my second book.

To the Surrey Fire Service Family, we are made up of Firefighters, Dispatchers, Support Staff and Chief Officers, a massive thanks to all of you. When I was hired in 1990, it was the best thing that had ever happened to me. I have made many lifelong friends who have stuck with me through thick and thin. I am proud to be a member of one of the best Fire Departments in North America.

Steve Serbic is an Assistant Fire Chief with the Surrey Fire Service.

He is not a clinical counsellor or psychologist but a concerned first responder advocating for change to workplace mental health policy. Any opinions expressed in this book, website, or podcast are his own drawn from personal experience. His websites are: SteveSerbic.com and MuscularMentalHealth.com featuring the podcast: Undercover Mental Health available on iTunes and Spotify

If you are struggling, please remember that help is available.
People do care, and you are not alone.
Dial: 988 **or Text:** 741741
(Available 24/7 daily across Canada and US)
US: National Suicide Prevention Lifeline 1-800-273-8255
Crisis Canada Services: 1-833-456-4566
Crisis Line UK: Text: 85258 / Call 0800 068 4141

Author – Steve Serbic spends his time living between Vancouver and Victoria, British Columbia, Canada with his wife and two kids.
To learn more visit SteveSerbic.com